REMNANTS
OF THE GODS

REMNANTS OF THE GODS

A Visual Tour of Alien Influence in
Egypt, Spain, France, Turkey, and Italy

By Erich von Däniken

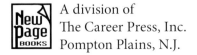

A division of
The Career Press, Inc.
Pompton Plains, N.J.

REMNANTS OF THE GODS
Edited and Typeset by Diana Ghazzawi
Cover illustration by noir33
Cover design by Howard Grossman/12E Design
Printed in the U.S.A.

Photo credits: Images 36 and 38, Albert Wyss; Images 55–59, Hartwig Hausdorf; Image 70, Peter Hentschel; Images 129, 149, 175–177 Ali Zarei; Image 155, Sandro Vannini; Images 156–157, Dassault Systèmes. All other images © Erich von Däniken, CH-3803-Beatenberg /Schweiz

To order this title, please call toll-free 1-800-CAREER-1 (NJ and Canada: 201-848-0310) to order using VISA or MasterCard, or for further information on books from Career Press.

The Career Press, Inc.
220 West Parkway, Unit 12
Pompton Plains, NJ 07444
www.careerpress.com
www.newpagebooks.com

Library of Congress Cataloging-in-Publication Data
CIP Available Upon Request

CONTENTS

Letter to My Readers

7

Impossible Buildings

9

Crazy Facts

71

False Doctrines

111

Notes

201

Index

211

About the Author

219

LETTER TO MY READERS

At some point in the obscure churning stew of prehistory, civilisations were at work on earth about which we do not have the faintest idea. Where did they come from? Where did they go? Why did they leave unfathomable buildings behind which make us shake our heads when we look at their ruins? What was actually going on unknown millennia ago? Why did the people of those times do what they did? Whom did they serve? Who directed them? Who were their gods? Why is no writing found either inside or outside their stone marvels? After all, at least the architects of the time must have had command of some form of writing. Without it, extensive complexes are not conceivable. What complexes? What—you may well ask!—am I going on about?

We are talking about buildings without history, cultures about which we know nothing, although they have left conspicuous traces behind. This applies not only to the stone circles and subterranean complexes, but also the large pyramids of Egypt. Little of what people try to tout as serious scientific thinking is correct. Scratch the surface, and we are left with unbridgeable contradictions and an earth-shattering naivety among the experts. On top of that, we have something simply inconceivable, something which should not exist—and yet covers our landscape. Demonstrable, measurable, checkable for everyone. Large parts of Europe lie under a geometric grid: I mean whole chains of original buildings which, without exception, are the same distance from one another, across hundreds of kilometers. These pseudo holy sites were slumbering there as long ago as the Stone Age, planned precisely by someone or other. Shaking our heads, looking the other way, or ignoring them will not make these points disappear off the map. They exist whether it suits the academic and public circus or not, and I appreciate every professor of surveying who finally decided to take a closer look at this incredible reality.

This is another volume in a five-volume series about the impossibilities of prehistory. This book is concerned with the large geographical areas surrounding the Mediterranean and the countries in its orbit. Every volume is intended to have 160–200 pictures and 100 pages of text. At the end, that will produce 1,000 pictures and 500 pages of text. The work as a whole should be understood as an updated digest of the wealth of information in many of my books. Repetition is intentional; without it, my new readers would be left dangling. Yet—and this is what makes the five-volume series so explosive—the most recent discoveries have brought current knowledge to a boiling point. The contradictions scream to high heaven. The forest of question marks keeps growing.

IMPOSSIBLE BUILDINGS

A hundred kilometers southwest of where the city of Tangier is located in Morocco today, at the western entrance to the Strait of Gibraltar, the Carthaginians in the seventh century BC built an ancient port city. They called it Lixus, "the eternal one." But this Lixus was built on top of the gigantic blocks of another, older, Phoenician city called Liks. The Phoenicians, in turn, had settled there as long ago as about 1200 BC. Not on a whim, for the Phoenicians—the great seafarers of antiquity—had come across the remains of a megalithic civilization in the same place. They made use of that. Those unknown megalithic people, the original builders of what later became Lixus, must have handled the imposing stone blocks as little Jimmy handles his toys. **(Images 1–4)** The harbour breakwater was as good as lined with colossal stone blocks, and the ramparts were built of hundreds of huge, partly cut granite rocks. If we want to understand how impossible that is, we should briefly consider that every technology follows a fixed evolutionary pattern. At the beginning, the simple people who have just descended from the trees learn how to handle wood and small stones. Then we get the first modest tools and primitive working of stone. Next comes the dressing of the raw blocks and their planning into larger structures. At length, some sort of transport is invented and tested, followed by the manufacture of fibers into pulleys or similar constructs. Finally, the human masses are divided and organised.

1

2

3

4

In Lixus, this "natural evolution of technology" is turned on its head. At the beginning, there was an ancient, unknown culture with the ready-made knowledge about how to work and transport extraordinary stones. Then, at some point in the course of the millennia, came the Phoenicians, followed later by the Carthaginians and, finally, the Romans. All these subsequent civilizations used the ready-made blocks from that unknown mysterious people, who at some point thought up and built this complex. (Carthage itself was totally destroyed by the Romans in 146 BC.)

Thor Heyerdahl, the famous experimental archaeologist, started his Atlantic voyage with the papyrus boat "RA" north of Lixus, and for good reason: that is where there is the strong flow of the Canary Current which carries vessels to Central America with minimal effort. Heyerdahl had not lost his sense of awe. He wrote about the megaliths of Lixus:

> Stones cut in various sizes and shapes, but always with vertical and horizontal sides and corners which fit exactly into one another like the stones of a giant jigsaw puzzle; even when the blocks displayed so many right-angled irregularities that the outlines could have been decagonal and dodecagonal instead of right-angled.[1]

Outside the city center of Lixus, whole ramparts of overgrown, curious stone formations lie about, which at first sight look like broken natural rock, but are not. Every more-detailed examination reveals that they have been artificially worked and precisely cut. (Images 5–8) Down at the beach at low tide, the blocks of a former breakwater can still be found; they do not originate from the Romans or the Carthaginians, let alone the Phoenicians. The archaeologist Gert von Hassler writes about them (Images 9–11):

> Thus the original walls of an Atlantic port have been preserved which occupies an important place in our collection of curiosities. Its stone blocks can neither be argued out of existence nor shifted in time. Lixus is definite: not a Moroccan fishing village, not a Roman temple square, not a Phoenician trading post. A prehistoric seaport.[2]

In his *Natural History*, the historian Pliny the Elder (AD 23–79) recounts that the original Lixus had once been a temple of Hercules.[3] This temple was surrounded by the much sought-after Garden of the Hesperides. The Hesperides were singing nymphs and, as the Greek poet Homer (c. 800 BC) recounts, also daughters of the gods Atlas and Zeus.[4] In addition to their daily singing, these graceful ladies also had to guard a grove with golden

6

7

9

10

11

12

16

17

18

19

20

21

22

apples. That went dreadfully wrong. Together with the nymphs, there lived in the Garden of the Hesperides a serpent called Ladon. The task of this reptile was actually to protect the beautiful nymphs, but the inevitable happened. The mighty Hercules, one of the heroes of the Greek *Argonautica*[5] (story of the capture of the Golden Fleece), killed the serpent.

What has any of this to do with Lixus? The story about the origins of Lixus digs deep into matters mythological. The elements of the beautiful, seductive nymphs, the serpent, and the stolen apples is interrelated with the Biblical story of Paradise, with Adam and Eve and the fatal bite out of the apple.

Was Lixus the same as the Biblical Garden of Eden? A paradise created by a god to raise the first humans? The most ancient stonework in Lixus was undertaken by a civilization of which we know nothing at all.

Today there is little left to see of the original Liks. It is difficult for the tourist to trace a few ruins of even the Roman Lixus. The place lies about three kilometers north of the Moroccan town of Larache, on the motorway

23

from Tangier to Rabat. The river Loukos winds its way toward the Atlantic Ocean. **(Image 12)** The banks of the river are a popular bathing beach. A golf course and modern settlement are being built just a kilometer away—part of it on the land of the ancient Lixus. On a hill overlooking the river, there are the remains of a Roman amphitheatre **(Images 13–14)**, a temple to Neptune and, in between on the hillside facing toward the river, ruins from that unknown age. Monolithic longitudinal and transverse blocks are still recognizable today which, although they were used by the Romans, were not their original building materials. The Romans used whatever happened to be lying about. **(Images 15–16)** And at the harbour breakwater on the Atlantic, there is a jumble of mighty blocks where it is difficult to see what was scattered by the roaring breakers and what was artificially processed in ages past.

About 30 kilometers north of Lixus, between the towns of Larache and Tétouan, the stone ellipse of Mzora lies on a hill. (It's also written "M'Soura," "M'Zora," or "Msoura.") The complex is difficult to find. Not a signpost far and wide. The ellipse consists of 167 monoliths and is surrounded by a

25

rampart. **(Images 17–22)** The longitudinal axis is 58 meters, the width 54 meters. A five-meter-high obelisk towers at the western entrance. Artificial incisions can be identified on individual blocks. **(Images 23–25)** No one knows what they mean, just as no one has the faintest idea who planted the megalithic ellipse of Mzora in the landscape, when it happened, and why. But Mzora is just the first of the impossible facts. The list gets more and more unendurable.

A tourist traveling from Granada, Spain, along the N342 (or from Malaga, the N331) toward Antequera should take the opportunity for an educational break and stop just before reaching Antequera. That is where the megalithic super graves of Menga, Viera, and el Romeral are located. Curiously, the Menga complex is described as *Cueva de Menga*, cave of Menga. Yet there is no natural cave. The Cueva de Menga is deemed to be "the most impressive and best preserved dolmen in the world."[6, 7] The alleged "cave" lies outside the town of Antequera and is described as a mausoleum in the specialist literature, although no corpse has ever been

26

found in it. This Stone Age miracle is 25 meters long, 5.5 meters wide, and 3.2 meters high—big enough to drive a tractor about. (**Images 26–28**)

No one knows who first entered this artificial structure because, until 1842, the dark space served as a cool chamber for keeping fruit and vegetables. Of course, people started to dig—twice even, in the years 1842 and 1874. The results did not yield any clues as to who built it. A renewed attempt was made in 1904; after all, there had to be something to find in this giant dolmen. The hard-pressed soil finally revealed a discus-shaped stone structure, whose purpose is unknown. No body, no bones, no sarcophagus, but below the ceiling there are some cross-shaped engravings and a five-pointed star with a diameter of about 18 centimeters.

The ceiling is a miracle in itself. The rear-most stone is 8.07 meters long and 6.3 meters wide. It has an estimated weight of 180 tonnes—certainly no lightweight. The actual "burial chamber," which never existed, is covered by four monolithic slabs resting on mighty stone supports. Each of these

27

28

lateral load-bearing stones is a good meter thick, the covering slabs more than twice that. All of it just a little bit massive for nothing. Anyone who moves and raises such monstrous stones might have taken care to ensure that the content of the tomb would stand the test of time. Or at least might have attached a little signature from the builders.

All the building materials of the Cueva de Menga consist of hard, tertiary Jura limestone quarried nearby at Cerro de la Cruz, no more than a kilometer away. That might not be a great distance, but still well-nigh impossible when transporting a slab weighing 180,000 kilograms! All the monoliths of Cueva de Menga are anchored into the ground with smaller stones. The surveyor of the clan must have attended an outstanding school of Stone Age architecture. Yet the Cueva de Menga is no more than a small step into the land of the impossible.

The limestone mountain Cuevas del Rey Moro, "caves of the black king," lies in the west of the province of Valencia in Spain; on its summit there is a megalithic town. Like Cueva de Menga, it is also called "Menga" although it lies somewhere completely different. The strange part about Menga is probably not mentioned by any classical historian because no one knows who built it and no one understands what in the world happened there millennia ago. Around the town of Menga, there is a "tram network" with "rails"—not rails from our time, but the remains of tracks that look like tramlines imprinted into the stone to a depth of 15 to 20 centimeters.[8] Yet the "tracks" near Menga are not unique either.

The town of Cyrene lies 400 meters above sea level in the barren desert south of the cities of Benghazi and Tobruk, in present-day Libya. As the teacher and writer Uwe Topper reports, legend says that it was built by a giant called Battos.[9] He must also have been pushing carts, because the tracks cannot be missed. Near the city of Cadiz in Spain, too, every tourist can see tracks of about 100 meters in length in the water at low tide. There are several.

And on the sunny Mediterranean island of Sardinia, the attentive visitor will stumble over numerous tracks. Even better, the island of Malta is covered in them. It goes against the grain to raise all of this old hat again, because I have reported about Malta in several books.[10, 11] Hence long-winded repetition is superfluous. Moreover, the pictures speak convincingly on their own.

29

34

Every attentive tourist in Malta will sooner or later see the "cart ruts," as the Maltese call them. Once again, these are railway track–like grooves in the ground, which could not have been tracks because the they are of different widths. **(Images 29–33)** Southwest of the old capital Mdina, near Dingli, the grooves in the ground accumulate and appear to be coming from everywhere, as at a railway junction. That is why the area is called "Clapham Junction" (a busy railway junction in London). These really are strange tracks: they pass through valleys and climb up hills. Frequently, several run alongside one another and suddenly converge into a double track before abruptly taking audacious bends. **(Images 34–38)** On several stretches of coast, such as St. Georg's Bay, south of Dingli, and Marsaxlokk Bay, the tracks go purposefully into the blue waters of the Mediterranean. **(Images 39–41)** The Malta researcher Alexander Knörr discovered whole collections of tracks that go under the water.[12] Then they suddenly end at a sharp drop. There must have been a rock slide, including the tracks, at such places. **(Image 42)**

36

37

38

There is plenty of speculation about this Maltese riddle. Were they cart ruts, skids of sledges? Roller bearings? Did the original inhabitants of Malta put their loads on a kind of forked branch and drag them across the countryside with draught animals? No good. The forked branch would have been too rigid and would not have changed the width of the tracks. Anyway, in that case, the tracks of the animals who pulled the heavy loads should also be evident in the limestone rock. But they aren't. Or—as the researcher André Schubert proposes—are the tracks in reality the traces of quite ordinary vehicles which only drove along the route once but on what was then soft ground?[13]

There has certainly been plenty of speculation. The "tracks" were a cult... a calendar... a conduit system... writing.... We are flooded with clever and, indeed, logical explanations, and yet an ultimate answer which is beyond any doubt is still missing. I consider the Maltese tracks to be a classic case of archaeological misconception and will explain why nothing can add up: Malta must never be looked at in isolation. Whatever this unknown

39

civilization in past millennia might have been, it was—as we have to realize today—transnational. It was connected with the whole Mediterranean area, including the adjacent regions, from North Africa to Britain, from Spain to Egypt. Track-like grooves in the ground can also be found in Sicily, Italy, Sardinia, Greece, southern France, Spain, Portugal, Turkey, and so on. The timeframe in which these incredible things happened is not 2,000 to 3,000 years BC, but a good 10,000 years ago or more. Today we know nothing about that time; there are no archaeologists at any university who are studying these things. Although "pre- and early history" is still taught at individual universities, it is without exception restricted to tiny geographical areas. Something like a comprehensive overview over the whole of Europe and beyond appears to be taboo. People are valiantly investigating their own little region. Giant spaces do not fit into the concept.

41

42

43

44

45

47

48

In Europe alone, there are several hundred stone and wood circles from the unknown past, and although no magazine called *Megalithic Today* existed at the time, all of these circles have an astronomical orientation. And all were designed using the same unit, the so-called Megalithic yard of 82.9 centimeters.[14] Who cares? Several of these complexes lie under water. For example, columns of menhirs lie off the island of Gavrini in Brittany; two stone circles are also snoozing there at a depth of 12 meters under the Atlantic. Tracks near Cadiz, in Malta, or on Sardinia lead into the water. And nowhere is there a science in sight that cares about that. What a superficial lot we have become! A society, moreover, that imagines that, thanks to the Internet, it is the best informed. Forget it!

Who, apart from the intelligent disbelievers and doubters who are interested by the mysteries of the world, has ever heard of a "hypogeum"? The word comes from the Greek and means "below the earth" (*hypo* meaning "below" and *gaia* meaning "earth"). The Hypogeum of Malta is just as mysterious as the tracks on the surface. The space was discovered purely by chance. In 1902, a builder found a stone slab in the ground near the quay wall of the large port of Malta which did not fit there. He levered it up and peered down into a rectangular shaft which disappeared vertically into the depths. The builder kept silent. He knew that there were subterranean complexes all over the island. He also kept his mouth shut because he feared the authorities might block his building plans. Today the underground chambers have been opened up to tourists—with restrictions. Groups wanting to visit the Hypogeum have to register in advance. Guests are first taken into a cinema where they can admire impressive pictures of the rock chambers. Then they can go in single file along a prescribed ramp to view a part of the complex. The Hypogeum is different from any other dolmen elsewhere in the world, different from the royal tombs in Egypt. Passageways branch off the main chamber to niches and smaller chambers. (**Images 43–44**) Walls and ceiling have been worked in perfect Megalithic style: clear lines and sharp edges on mighty blocks. Above them is a rounded, curved ceiling in three layers, one above the other. (**Images 45–46**) A total work of art, it is a masterpiece which does not fit into the Stone Age at all. The monoliths extend smoothly from the floor to the ceiling, the niches have been flawlessly hammered out of the rock, the curved ceiling even in the form of a dome. That is totally alien to Stone Age thinking. (**Images 47–48**) Who chiselled this complex out of the rock? What was it for?

49

It is the same as at Lixus. It was not the Romans, Greeks, or Phoenicians, because the Hypogeum had long been in existence in their time. The Greeks were just as unaware of the complex lying up to 12 meters underground as the Romans. From the rear-most chamber of the Hypogeum, a shaft leads into unknown depths, in which up to 7,000 skeletons are said to have been found. I cannot check whether this is true.

The Stone Age is called the Stone Age because people worked with stones. They did not know metals. Flint, at minimum, would have been required to chisel the Hypogeum out of the rock. It is harder than limestone. But there is no flint on Malta. The guidebooks for tourists say the Hypogeum had been built in three phases. It may well be true that in later periods (whenever that may have been!) natural niches in the rock were extended and smoothed, but this has nothing to do with the main chamber and the curved, domed ceiling. "These chambers display a symmetry

50

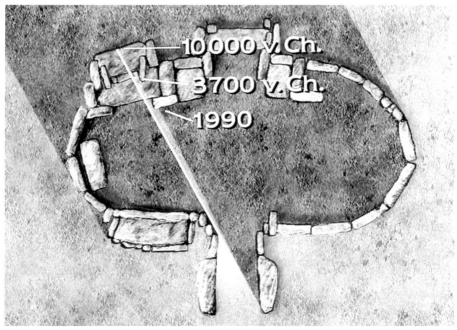

51

52

53

54

in their construction which has no equal," the Malta specialist Alexander Knörr writes.[15] "Furthermore, the chambers have impressive acoustics. Words whispered into an oracle hole can be loudly and clearly heard in the whole complex." Once again, Stone Age geniuses were at work here whose methods we cannot even begin to fathom. The academic discipline that should take responsibility refuses to include these things in its research program, and so the impossible is suppressed. The same applies to the 30 megalithic temples on the island, whereby at least the temple of Mnajdra can be shown to be at least 12,000 years old. How is that possible? **(Images 49–50)**

The cartographer Paul Micallef, used to precision work by nature of his job, made an astonishing discovery during the survey work in Mnajdra.[16] The whole Mnajdra complex looks like a trefoil with a diameter of about 70 meters. The temple has an astronomical orientation. On the day of the summer solstice, precisely at sunrise, a beam of light shines from the right entrance monolith into the oval chamber behind. There it throws a small, vertical beam of light on to a block standing on the left side. But that was

not always the case. At about 3700 BC, the beam went past the monolith and touched the edge of a stone lying further back; 10,000 years BC, it was different again. At that time, the beam of light precisely hit the center of the altar stone lying even further back. At the winter solstice on December 21, the spectacle repeated itself except from the opposite side. But there is no altar stone there. Sounds complicated.

That there is no coincidence involved is shown by the alignment of the temple with the dates of the spring and autumn equinox. How is it possible to read a date of 12,000 years from this natural play of the light? This is where we get to the exciting bit and **Images 51–54** prove it: Depending on whether it is the winter or summer solstice, a column of light is created on the monolith lying behind on the *right* or *left* side. The right-hand monolith measures 1.33 meters in width, the left-hand one 1.2 meters. The light columns can easily be read off the right monolith; after all, we know what line is created at the winter solstice of *our* century. The column of light circuits the whole stone once in the course of 25,800 years. Its width signals the start of the whole spectacle: 10,205 BC. That this number is difficult to digest for my friends the pre-historians is understandable. The date completely upsets the whole much-loved categorisation of our Stone Age ancestors. But it is of little value in any case, as I will go on to show.

If hitherto we have always learnt that religious culture started in Mesopotamia with the Sumerians, followed later by the Babylonians, Egyptians, and a few others, this school of thought is wrong again. In southeastern Turkey, about 15 kilometers northeast of the provincial capital Şanliurfa, excavations are underway at Göbekli Tepe, which once again call into question the natural evolution of technology, as they do of spirituality. Göbekli Tepe, incidentally, means "potbelly hill" in the local language, and according to legend, the patriarch Abraham is said to have been born in the nearby city of Şanliurfa. A circular temple complex was uncovered in which three rings of walls enclose a center. **(Images 55–56)** There are monoliths which remind us of seating, and at the edge of the inner circle there are T-shaped stone columns, weighing up to 16 tonnes, with individual incisions on them—circles, half-moons, and a carving similar to our letter "H." We can also admire stone carvings of foxes, lions, snakes, gazelles, and cranes. **(Images 57–59)** All the T-shaped crossbeams on top of the monoliths are aligned toward the center of the complex. So far, three of these ring-shaped complexes have been uncovered. Yet geomagnetic measurements have

61

62

revealed the existence of at least 20 other stone circles. A mere 10 percent of the structures lying under the ground have been recorded. All in all, a difficult lump to digest: it has been determined to be 11,500 years old. Who in the obscurity of that distant past built not just one, but several stone circles directly next to one another? Weren't we always taught that the fur-clad numpties of the time had been fully occupied with foraging for food and keeping wild animals at bay? Reality speaks a different language. Another incomprehensible thing: the builders are said to have reburied their stone rings intentionally and at a time of peace. Not simultaneously. They buried one of their complexes and then started building another circle nearby. "What is the meaning of that?" the archaeological writer Hartwig Hausdorf enquires. "Did [the builders] want to preserve the unique complex for the people of the future? What message did they want to send us?"[17]

Nothing is impossible. I cannot, however, see why a civilization would carefully bury its holy sites, if that is what they were, in sand and rubble for the people of the future. After all, they could not know whether their complexes would ever be discovered again. I consider another variant to be more likely: they buried their structures in order to prevent anyone being harmed in them. Had a deadly disease broken out which they could not control? In Leviticus, the Lord gives precise instructions from chapter 14 onward about what should be done in the case of infectious diseases—up to and including the destruction of the affected buildings.[18] The fact is that Göbekli Tepe was gradually and carefully buried again by someone, and it happened about 8,000 years ago.

The location of Göbekli Tepe is also a curiosity. Why here? What was so important about this geographic site? After all, the builders needed water but the nearest river lies five kilometers away. What important event turned this location into holy ground, a spiritual site for the community? Some religious thought must have united the people. Perhaps the patriarch Abraham can help; after all, the place of his birth, today's city of Şanliurfa, lies only about 15 kilometers away. Something extraordinary did indeed happen in Abraham's immediate environment millennia ago. It is told in the *Apocalypse of Abraham.*[19]

There an eyewitness tells in the first person how the boy Abraham was working one evening in his father Baruch's garden. We learn how two "heavenly beings" descended to earth.[20] The two of them grabbed the boy Abraham and dragged him "to the edge of the flames." Incidentally,

Abraham is quite specific that they were not human, because they did "not have human breath" and they "sparkled all over their bodies like sapphire." Then the smoke and fire opened up, and the sparkly characters ascended with Abraham "as if with many winds." Up there, Abraham sees "from the heights we had climbed something like a powerful, indescribable light" and finally large figures who spoke words to one another "which I did not understand." Next, the youth Abraham notes succinctly and unequivocally where he is: "But I wished to travel down to earth. The high place where we stood was sometimes upright but then it turned downward."[21]

We should savor this statement. Here we have someone reporting from ancient times, written down in the first person, that after his journey toward the sky he had wished to descend *downward to earth*. He must logically have been *outside* the earth. Furthermore, Abraham must have been in a spaceship in orbit around the earth. Why? Because "the high place where we stood" is rotating around its axis: *"was sometimes upright but then it turned downward."* Every spaceship in orbit rotates constantly around its own axis because such rotation creates a centrifugal force inside it: artificial gravity. Not something a Stone Age person could have known—unless he experienced it on his own body.

This is just one suggestion for the archaeologists searching for a spiritual event to explain the mystery of Göbekli Tepe. The *Apocalypse of Abraham* describes a sensational, plausible reason for the inconceivable. After all, "Abraham's ascension" started in the garden of his father Baruch, and he lived directly next to "potbelly hill" called Göbekli Tepe.

There are thousands of granite blocks—so-called menhirs—in Brittany which are set up in geometrical lines.[22, 23] They form Pythagorean triangles ($a^2 + b^2 = c^2$), and they did so millennia before Pythagoras. No professor of archaeology is interested. (**Images 60–63**) Straight lines are drawn across Europe over hundreds, sometimes thousands of kilometers. They connect Stone Age holy sites from Norway to Sicily, from Denmark to Greece— not something that is actually possible, because our ancestors would have had to survey the whole of Europe for that. But the impossible is a reality and has been proven without a shadow of a doubt.[24, 25, 26] The discoverers of such realities are ridiculed and mocked by society. There are neither honors nor prizes for them. No one takes responsibility: no foundation, no university, and no newspaper publisher, let alone a TV station. Cowardice, a lack of moral courage, rules. And all of us have become fellow travelers of

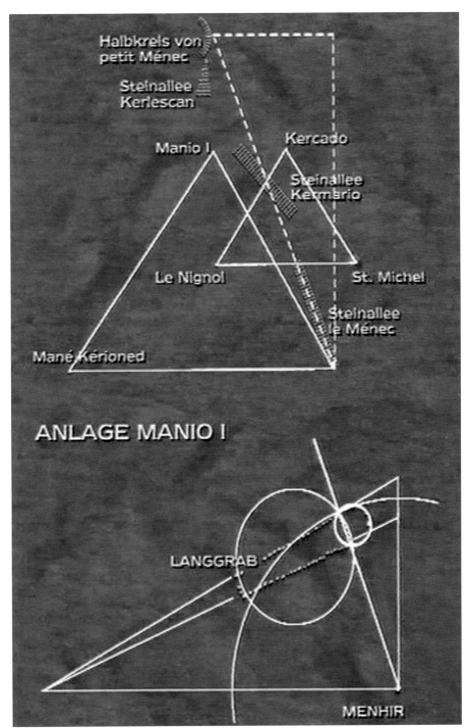

indifference. There are hundreds of dolmens in the Mediterranean region and just as many stone circles. The great majority of them have an astronomical orientation. Our society with its electronic stupification, could not care less. Stone Age? Lost civilizations? Of what relevance is our past to us? Yet incomprehensible facts lie below everyone's feet, so to speak, which do not fit into any conception of history or archaeological textbook. The absurd thing is that all these impossible facts about which I am about to report are childishly simple to check without any great effort. The only things that are required are a map, dividers, and a ruler. And in no time at all, ancient links on European soil become visible, links that should never have existed because they originate in that unknown, fairy-tale Stone Age over which there rises a stench of decay. The impossible is reported next.

CRAZY FACTS

"It seems as if the whole of northeastern Bavaria is covered by a network of such aerial lines...." These words come from Karl Bedal, who investigated a curious network of lines in his home region and rediscovered his sense of wonder.[1] "Millennia ago," the thorough Karl Bedal said, "the eastern part of Upper Franconia, that is, the Fichtel Mountains and Franconian Forest, was covered with impenetrable woods."[2] It was not until after the birth of Christ that farmers and monks arrived and began the clear the forest. So there *cannot* have been a network of lines in that hilly, Bavarian forest which links Stone Age points with one another. Make sense? Yet it does exist. Karl Bedal writes, "These are inexplicable straight lines which cross and intersect one another...always comprising a measure of 6.75 km or a multiple thereof, that is, 13.5 km, 27 km, up to 54 and 81 km and so on."[3]

The small town of Schesslitz is located in the Upper Franconian district of Bamberg (Bavaria, Germany). It is also known as the "gateway to Franconian Switzerland." Northwest of it, there is an ancient wooden cross called the Red Cross. A heathen cultic stone previously stood at the same spot. From the Red Cross, draw a straight line in a northeastern direction to Castle Peesten 27 kilometers away. Nothing special about that: two points can always be connected with a straight line. From Peesten, the line continues to Tennersreuth, 27 kilometers away—and another 27 kilometers to the Schönwald Stone near Schönwald. Up to this point, we have measured three times 27 kilometers as the crow flies, a total of 81 kilometers—this

71

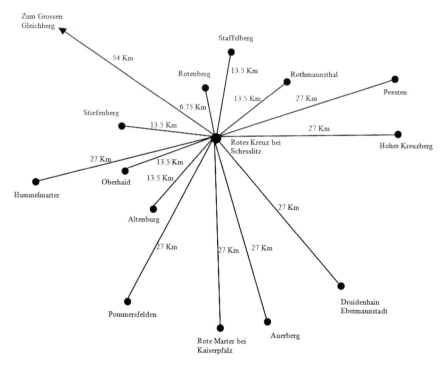

in hilly primeval forest. We started in Schesslitz. From there, lines radiate in all directions to target the following other points: Peesten (northeast), Hoher Kreuzberg (east), the druid grove Druidenhain at Ebermannstadt (southeast), Auerberg (south), the Rote Marter near Kaiserpfalz (south), Pommersfelden (southwest) and Hummelmarter (west). Every point is precisely 27 kilometers distant from Schesslitz. **(Image 64)**

What looks like a silly game turns out, on closer inspection, to be prehistoric planning. The town of Staffelstein lies north of Bamberg, and a short distance away from it, the Staffelberg mountain. From here, 27 kilometer-long lines radiate out to Rotheul, Haig, Veste Rosenberg, Burghaig, Schloss Thurnau, Hoher Kreuzberg, Unteraufsess, Heiligenstadt, Rothof (north of Bamberg) and Burgpreppach. That alone makes eleven points around the Staffelberg mountain, all of them 27 kilometers away. But this only scratches the surface of the inexplicable grid which indisputably lies over the landscape. In his pamphlet, which, incidentally, is published by the Historical Society of Upper Franconia, Karl Bedal flawlessly demonstrates

Calais
Mont Alix
Mont Alet
L'Allet
Anxon
Aisey
Alaise
L'Allex
Vercelli
Alzano
Calesi

Cales

the existence of a whole grid of ancient points which are all connected by dead-straight lines. The distances are always 27 kilometers, half of that (13.5 km) or a quarter (6.75 km). To quote Karl Bedal, "The whole system of lines is interlinked and connected, all crossing points and nodes are linked through other cross-connections."[4]

All just a game? Did Mr. Karl Bedal simply draw a few lines on a map and some places just happened to lie underneath? Definitely not. The straight lines and identical distances mean that any coincidence is absurd. What Mr. Bedal (and others) discovered in Germany was found by Monsieur Xavier Guichard in the same way in France. Our Mr. Guichard first held office as the chief of police in Paris, then studied philology, advanced to become the vice president of the French Society for Prehistory, and began to ask himself how many places there might be in France with the same root word in their name. So he started searching for places containing the word "Bourg," others with the root words "Flora" or "Calais." At the word "Alaise," his heart began to beat faster. Believe it or not, 382 place

names contained the same root word, and a further 47 places went back to "Calais." That could no longer be described as normal. Monsieur Guichard reached for a ruler and map. Many of the places lay under a straight line from the British Isles over the Alps to Sicily: Calais—Mont Alix—Mont Alet—L'Alet—Anxon—Aisey—Alaise—L'Alex—Alzano—Calesi—Cales, and so on. Here 24 lines from all points of the compass crossed at the village of Alaise. (**Image 65**) This place lies in the eastern Jura, northeast of Salin-les-Bains, just 70 kilometers away from the Swiss border—actually in the heart of Europe. The 24 lines that cross here run from Scotland to Corsica, from Great Britain to France, from Portugal to Germany. More and more parallel lines appeared. One of them intersected Carlisle and Ely in England, Calais and eight further names derived from Alaise in France, and went via Alasio and Calice in Italy to Aliso on Corsica. Xavier Guichard originally thought that the whole system of lines was based on the old "wind rose system." Before longitude and latitude were introduced, maps were made in accordance with the "wind rose system." A point was fixed, usually on a hill top, and lines were drawn from there in various directions. Someone then rode along those lines to measure the length of the ride from one point to the next. Cross-connections between the lines were also possible. But Guichard soon noticed that many lines had to be older than any wind rose system. Frequently the points were not just the same distance from one another, they also touched on places which were unknown in the early Middle Ages—for example, a Stone Age settlement under the waters of Lake Zurich near the town of Meilen. Rotten poles, bones, ceramics, and stone from a settlement thousands of years old were found there in the winter of 1854. Xavier Guichard's line went precisely over it. Furthermore, the wind rose system could not explain lines from England to Sicily. The linear distance is about 2,000 kilometers. And the prehistoric holy sites with the common root words—L'Allet, Alaise, L'Allex, and so on—existed long before the wind rose system was introduced. The philologist Guichard could not contain his surprise and noted, "There must at some point have existed a homogenous civilisation which was based on considerable scientific knowledge."[5]

Incidentally, the village of Alaise, where all the lines intersect, was a druid holy site as late as Roman times. In 47 BC, Julius Caesar defeated the Gallic tribes under Vercingetorix. (The latter even appears in *Asterix*.) The druids were clearly aware of the sacred nature of this "star point of Alaise."

Xavier Guichard traced the root of the word "Alaise" back to the Greek Elysion. Elysion (Greek) or Elysium (Latin) is regarded in Greek mythology as the Island of the Blessed. The heroes beloved of the gods were taken to Elysion—immortal for eternity. And today? Elysium is celebrated in the European anthem. In 1972, the Council of Europe and, in 1986, the European Union decided to adopt the "Ode to Joy" as the European anthem. The text is by the German poet philosopher, historian, and playwright Friedrich Schiller (1759–1805) and the music by no less a composer than Ludwig von Beethoven (1770–1827):

Freude, schöner Götterfunke,

Tochter aus Elysium,

Wir betreten feuertrunken,

Himmlische, dein Heiligtum.

Deine Zauber binden wieder,

Was die Mode streng geteilt,

Alle Menschen werden Brüder,

Wo dein sanfter Flügel weilt.

Joy, beautiful spark of the gods,

Daughter of Elysium,

In fiery intoxication we enter,

Heavenly one, thy holy sanctuary.

Thy magic power reunites

What custom has strictly parted,

All human beings become brothers

Under thy gentle wing.

The village of Alaise today consists of just 20 houses and an 11th century church, a sleepy farming village in the French Jura. **(Image 66)** There are the remains of Gaulish fortifications on the hills around Alaise. **(Images 67–68)** But what was there that needed defending in Alaise? The village historian, Monsieur Louis Courlet, explained to me that there were ancient graves from the Iron and Bronze Ages around Alaise which had often been robbed by earlier inhabitants. The graves contained tools and jewelry—a valuable raw material for the production of weapons. Today's inhabitants of Alaise and the surrounding villages know about the unique nature of the "star point" Alaise, and they know about the lines that converge on the village from all directions—yet no one has an explanation for the mystery. Courlet, who has written down the history of the village with incredible hard work and meticulousness,[6] expressed the view in a personal conversation that the secret of the lines probably had to be seen as one of the riddles of prehistory. Indeed, Monsieur Courlet has a small exhibition in two rooms in Alaise, which he is happy to show to tourists. Yet tourists rarely find their way to Alaise. Invisible lines cannot be looked at.

Human beings have been discovering things from the beginning. Behind every horizon, there is new knowledge; behind every molecule, new combinations of atoms; behind every atom, new sub-atomic particles, new waves. Human beings are learning to marvel again. One of these marveling people is the qualified engineer Peter Hentschel from Dresden, a man with patience, perseverance, and clear, analytical reason. Some years ago he spent some months with a friend in Tuscany in Italy and had no inkling of the mysterious lines in the landscape which would suddenly fascinate him, had no clue that he would be unexpectedly studying the Etruscans and even the Tree of Life of the Jewish Kabbalah. Peter Hentschel is a specialist in surveying. He thinks scientifically. The Etruscans and Kabbalah have about as much to do with his specialist area as an anteater with a crater on the moon. But things did not turn out as expected.

Engineer Hentschel was asked to help with the renovation of an old country house in Tuscany. A 12th-century church is part of the house, and it stands on the remains of an Etruscan cultic site. His friend drew his attention to a curiosity of the region. There was a straight line between the town of Anghiari (famous for the battle of Anghiari), the town of Arezzo, and a Franciscan monastery on Monte Casale. Part of the line is the straight road from Anghiari to San Polcro. What was that about? To begin with, Peter Hentschel shook his head in disbelief but then discovered confirmation in the landscape. A check with his GPS and a computer specially programmed for spherical trigonometry confirmed the information from his friend. But then he began to wonder. The monastery of Laverna lay at right angles to the north of Anghiari. It was the place at which St Francis of Assisi (1182–1226) received the stigmata. Strange. Had the Franciscan monks set up their monasteries in a geometrical pattern? Things were to become even more strange. Once again at right angles and at the same distance there was Petroja, a church of the Templars. Now the engineer's curiosity was aroused. Were there still other churches, chapels, or holy sites at the same distances?

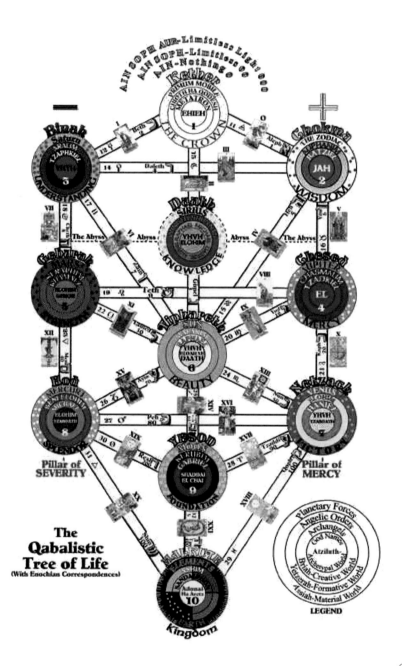

Peter Hentschel consulted maps and went to inspect his ever-more-curious discoveries on the ground with GPS and a digital camera. Gradually a system made up of a whole lot of equilateral triangles over the landscape crystalized, in which a distance of 74 kilometers, or exactly half of that, lay between one point and the next. The places were partly ancient Etruscan sites which had belonged to the 12-city Etruscan League, chapels, shrines to the Madonna, or remains of Etruscan walls. The Christian chapels often stood on the remains of Etruscan holy sites. An example: The distance from Cortona to a Bronze Age settlement on Lake Bolsena is 74 kilometers. A straight line can be drawn from both places to Paganaico. Both distances are, in turn, 74 kilometers. There are Marian chapels, Romanesque churches, or the remains of Etruscan walls at these points.

Often the distance from one point to another was 37 kilometers—half the distance of 74 kilometers. Peter Hentschel, the engineer specialising in surveying, transferred his findings to a map, which I reproduced with his permission. The result was a grid of more than 12 equidistant points. The whole system has a strict north–south orientation. (Places such as San Cristoforo, Corton, Citta della Pieve, Perugia, Todi, Orte, and Blera lie at the nodes.) And the middle line of this network lies precisely on the 12th parallel east. The image which was reproduced on the map was very like the Tree of Life in the Kabbalah. What is the Kabbalah's Tree of Life? **(Images 69–70)**

The word "Kabbalah" comes from the Hebrew *qabal*, "receive." (Hebrew QBLH means "what is received.") It may be that the content of the Kabbalah even goes back to Moses, as is claimed in Kabbalistic circles, but a fragment of the Kabbalah was written down by Rabbi Simon Bar Jochai (AD 130–170) as late as the second century AD. A thousand years later, the Spanish Jew Moses Ben Schemtob de Leon prepared the version which we have today as the comprehensive text of the Kabbalah.[7] It has been translated into several languages. According to these Kabbalistic writings, God revealed himself through emanations throughout the universe. The manifestations of God are called "Sephirot" and presented pictorially in a system which is called the "Kabbalistic Tree."[8] This "Tree" shows all the mystical spheres of the divine forces "and is an allegorical image of the form of the heavenly and perfect human being."[9]

Peter Hentschel's triangles in Tuscany reflect exactly this Kabbalistic Tree of Life. Coincidence? Who in the past would have had the power to

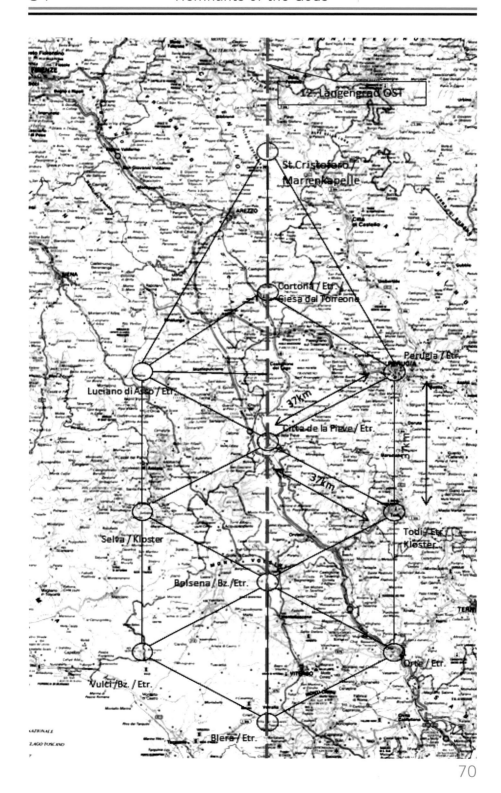

plant such an over-dimensional image, consisting of sacred corner points, into the landscape? The question remains unanswered. During the eight years he spent studying this astonishing geometry, Peter Hentschel quite separately discovered a highly puzzling geometrical network spread across the whole of central Italy which definitively had to be older than the brothers of the Franciscan order. They did not locate their holy places by accident, in any old place, but kept to the existing sacred points from the time of the Etruscans.

Central Italy was the land of the Etruscans about 3,000 years ago. Where they came from has not been explained to the present day. Herodotus, the Greek "father of history," reports that the Etruscans were migrants from Lydia in Asia Minor.[10] As early as in the eighth century BC, the Etruscans maintained intensive trade with Greece, and their religion was definitely influenced by the Greek world of the gods. Their priests knew the divine symbols and possessed, in particular, very precise surveying skills. Their urns were accordingly decorated with geometrical motifs. But the knowledge of the Etruscan priests about geometry came from ancient Greece. This claim can be proved easily.

Here are the facts I have reported on several occasions without ever having received a response from the scientific establishment.[11, 12, 13]

In the autumn of 1974, I gave a lecture to the Rotary Club in Athens. At the end of the discussion, a bald gentleman with graying temples approached me and enquired politely whether I was aware that most of the Greek holy sites were connected in a geometrical relationship. I smiled and said I found that difficult to imagine because the ancient Greeks did not, after all, possess geodetic surveying techniques. Furthermore, I objected, the temples were often many kilometers apart and the Greek mountains meant there was no direct line of sight between one holy site and another. Finally, I considered in a know-it-all manner, the classical sites were also on islands hundreds of kilometers distant from the mainland and cannot be seen with the naked eye in any case. I was thinking of the distance to Crete or Izmir, Turkey, the Smyrna of the Stone Age. So, what was the friendly gentleman going on about?

We met again two days later, this time at the military airport of Athens. Maps and aeronautical charts had been spread out on a large table. The bald gentleman introduced himself: Dr Theophanias Manias, brigadier in the Greek air force. Why was this military big cheese interested in archaeology? He explained it to me over a cup of tea.

71

72

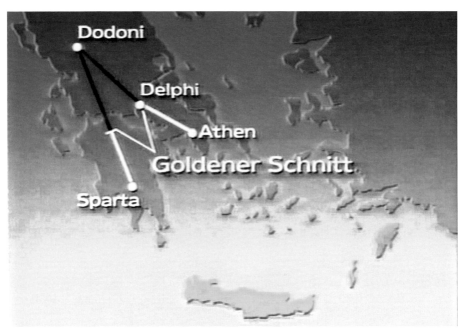

73

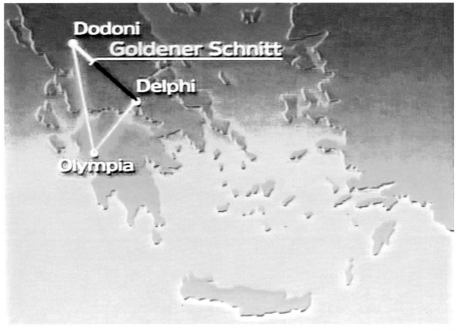

74

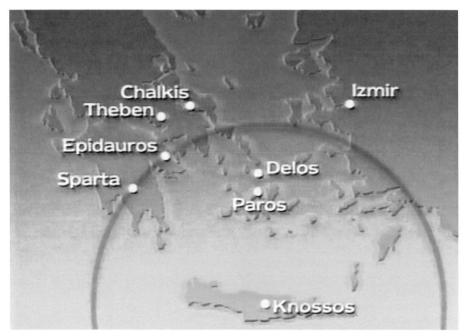

75

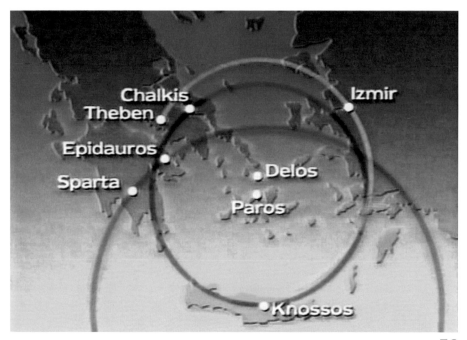

76

It was normal practice, he said, for the military pilots to undertake surveillance and training flights in the mountains or target practice over the sea. Afterward, they had to prepare a report which also recorded fuel consumption. In the course of the years, a lieutenant who had transferred the data into a table noticed that the same fuel quantities and distances kept being cited, although the pilots had flown in different areas. The lieutenant thought he had discovered a fiddle. The pilots were too lazy to enter the correct information in their log books, and so they copied from one another. Thus the dossier ended up on the desk of Colonel Manias. (He only became brigadier at a later date.)

Mr. Manias took dividers, placed the point on Delphi, and drew a circle over the Acropolis. Curiously, the circle also touched Argos and Olympia. Then the brigadier placed the tip of the dividers on Knossos in Crete. The circle also touched Sparta und Epidaurus—strange. Center of the circle Delos: Thebes and Izmir also lay on it. Center of the circle Paros: Knossos and Chalcis also lay on it. Center of the circle Sparta: Mycenae and the classical oracle of Trofonion also lay on it.

Dr. Manias handed me three documents in English, Spanish, and German, all with the same content.[14, 15, 16] They had been prepared with the active support of the military geographic office in Athens and published by the Association for Operational Research. From them I learned and anyone can check (**Images 71–76** "Goldener Schnitt" is the golden ratio.):

- The distance between the cultic sites of Delphi and Epidaurus corresponds to the larger section of the golden ratio for the distance from Epidaurus to Delos, specifically 62%.

- The distance between Olympia and Chalkis corresponds to the larger section of the golden ratio for the distance from Olympia to Delos, specifically 62%.

- The distance between Delphi and Thebes corresponds to the larger section of the golden ratio for the distance from Delphi to the Acropolis, specifically 62%.

- The distance between Delphi and Olympia corresponds to the larger section of the golden ratio for the distance from Olympia to Chalcis, specifically 62%.

- The distance between Epidaurus and Sparta corresponds to the larger section of the golden ratio for the distance from Epidaurus to Olympia, specifically 62%.

- The distance between Delos and Eleusis corresponds to the larger section of the golden ratio for the distance from Delos to Delphi, specifically 62%.
- The distance between Knossos and Delos corresponds to the larger section of the golden ratio for the distance from Knossos to Chalcis, specifically 62%.
- The distance between Delphi and Dodoni corresponds to the larger section of the golden ratio for the distance from Delphi to the Acropolis, specifically 62%.
- The distance between Sparta and Olympia corresponds to the larger section of the golden ratio for the distance from Sparta to the Acropolis, specifically 62%.

Yet there is method in this madness. What is the probability that in mountainous terrain three temples happen to lie on a straight line? It might happen in two or three cases. In Attica and Boeotia (central Greece) alone there are 35 of these "three-temple lines." Tuscany salutes!

What is the probability that the linear distances between holy sites is the same? It happens 22 times in central Greece. Coincidence? Hardly.

And Delphi, the "navel of the world," plays the role of the hub airport in this network. Thus Delphi is the same distance from the Acropolis and Olympia. We can construct a perfect equilateral triangle. The holy site of Nemea lies at the half-way point of the cathetus (one of the two shorter legs of a right-angled triangle). The right-angled triangles of Acropolis–Delphi–Nemea and Nemea–Delphi–Olympia have the same hypotenuse, and its ratio to the common Delphi–Nemea line corresponds to the golden ratio.

And now things get even more peculiar: the distance from Delphi to Aphea is the same as from Aphea to Sparta. The distance from Delphi to Sparta is the same as the distance from Sparta to Thebes and—incidentally—also half the distance of the line from Dodoni to Sparta and Dodoni to the Acropolis. The distances are also the same for Delphi–Mycenae and Mycenae–Athens or Delphi–Gortys (a megalithic ruin on Crete) and Delphi–Milet in Asia Minor. In summary, Delphi is geodetically and geometrically related to Olympia, Dodoni, Eleusis, Epidaurus, Aphea, the Acropolis, Sparta, Mycenae, Thebes, Chalcis, Nemea, Kinyra, Gortys, and Milet.

78

To complete this madness, we still need to swallow the following: Everyone can imagine an equilateral triangle. But in ancient Greece, there is evidence of several triangles with two proportions relating to the different leg lengths. It works as follows. Take the triangle Dodoni–Delphi–Sparta: the places have the same leg ratio as Dodoni–Sparta to Dodoni–Delphi, Dodoni–Sparta to Sparta–Delphi, and Dodoni–Delphi to Delphi–Sparta.

The triangle Knossos–Delos–Chalcis: the places have the same leg ratio as Knossos–Chalcis to Knossos–Delos, Knossos–Chalkis to Chalkis–Delos, and Knossos–Delos to Delos–Chalcis.

The triangle Nicosia (Cyprus)–Knossos (Crete)–Dodoni: the places have the same leg ratio as Nicosia–Dodoni to Nicosia–Knossos, Nicosia–Dodoni to Dodoni–Knossos, and Nikosia zu Knossos–Dodoni.

All these triangles are the same. With the assistance of the military geographic office, more than 200 geometric equivalent ratios were nailed down. An additional 148 proportions based on the golden ratio can be added to them. To keep talking about coincidence is absurd. After all, we are not just talking about names on a map but cultic sites from antiquity—or to be

79

precise, prehistory. Thus the temple of Apollo in classical Delphi stands on foundations from the Stone Age. **(Images 77–79)**

Professor Fritz Rogowski from the Technical University in Brunswick was the only academic far and wide to want to try and crack this nut of a puzzle. He did indeed find small stone circles here and there in the mountainous terrain of Greece. He looked around for further markers and, lo and behold, in several cases he discovered a second stone circle just within view.[17] Rogowski extended the lines of the marker points and—in multiple cases (!)—landed on a cultic site at the end of such a chain. Had the nut been cracked?

No. The lines in the Greece of antiquity bridged not just mountain ranges but also sea routes. One line of the Delphi–Olympia–Acropolis triangle bridges a 20-kilometer-long track across the sea. The same applies to Dodoni–Sparta. It becomes patently absurd in triangles such as Knossos–Delos–Argos. About 300 kilometers of sea lie between Knossos on Crete and Argos—not bridgeable with the naked eye.[18]

The clever academics of our day adhere to the principle of "simple probability," the "most obvious solutions." This principle prohibits them from

80

any other way of thinking. They cannot escape from their thought prison, because with the "most obvious solution," the problem has been dealt with. What else is there to investigate? This method, even if it is declared to be infallible by science, only provides half-answers for any but the most super-ficial problems. One of these non-solutions which lulls these minds hap-pily to sleep is derived from the knowledge of the mathematicians of Greek antiquity. Euclid lived in the third/fourth century BC and gave lectures in Egypt and Greece. He compiled several textbooks both on the full range of mathematics and on all of geometry, including proportions. Euclid was a contemporary of the philosopher Plato and he, in turn, was intermittently active as a politician. Thus Plato is said to have sat at the feet of Euclid and listened to his discourses on geometry. Is it not obvious that Plato was inspired by the explanations of the mathematical genius Euclid and made use of this geometrical knowledge when he discussed building projects in his capacity as a politician?

This honorable intellectual approach is worthless because all the sacred sites which come into question existed long before Euclid. Their origins go back far into prehistoric times, even for "ancient Greece." That applies to the Acropolis, Delos, Mycenae, and Epidaurus as much as to Knossos

81

on Crete. Every place was originally megalithic. **(Images 80–85)** At best, Euclid was passing on knowledge which was much older than he was himself. That is something which the few academics who study the mathematics of antiquity also know. Professor Neugebauer has compared Platonic geometry with Euclidean, and the latter with the geometry of Egypt and Assur.[19] His colleague Professor Jean Richter discovered a geometry in the temple layout in ancient Greece which had long been in existence in pre-Euclidean times.[20] The brilliant Greek mathematicians *cannot* have had anything to do with the geometrical arrangement of the holy sites because these locations were already sacred long before these mathematicians were born. Euclid, Plato, Pythagoras, and Socrates cannot help us further here. But *where* did this geometrical knowledge come from and why did the "ancient Greeks" arrange their sacred sites in accordance with geometrical patterns and equal distances? Plato—Euclid's listener—mentions whole series of geometrical connections in chapters seven and eight of his work *Timaeus.* He knew about the vast distances extending far beyond Greece and therefore warned, "Let no one ignorant of geometry have a say in this matter. Geometry is the knowledge of eternal existence."[21]

The facts are clear to see: precise, applied geometry in the thousands of menhirs near the town of Carnac in Brittany ($a^2+b^2=c^2$). Precise, applied geometry in the so-called ley lines which run across Europe. Precise, applied geometry not just in Franconia (Germany) but throughout Germany and beyond. Precise, applied geometry over a large territorial network of holy and secular points in Tuscany. Precise, applied geometry both in France and in ancient Britain. As long ago as 1870, the historian Henry Black, a member of the British Archaeological Association in London, declared, "Monuments exist marking grand geometrical lines, lines which cover the whole of the west of Europe, extending beyond Britain to Ireland, the Hebrides, the Shetlands, the Orkneys, right up to the Arctic circle.... [This system] exists in India, China and in the provinces of the east which are all laid out in the same way."[22] Precise geometry over the prehistoric temples in Greece. And this is only the tip of the iceberg. The New Zealander Bruce Cathie, professional pilot and former captain of a DC-8, in two books establishes a giant network of ancient lines which spread across the globe.[23, 24] A comparable network of lines also lies over South America. Books have been written about that which no one knows about.[25, 26, 27, 28] I myself deal with the subject in *Die Steinzeit war ganz anders,* p. 249ff. (The Stone Age was quite different).

We might be able to explain these things if the Stone Age people had somehow and somewhere marked their territories. But this simple explanation does not work. Just try measuring a straight line of 74 kilometers in dense forest overgrown with roots, ferns, and trees—and, moreover, in hilly terrain. In recent centuries, these areas were surveyed from one triangulation point (triangle) to the next; today it is done from the air or with satellites. What resources did the grunting prehistoric humans possess? And why, for heaven's sake, did our ancestors, who had hardly mutated into *Homo sapiens*, survey their lands both north and south of the Alps (Tuscany)? A tunnel through the Swiss Alps did not exist at the time, and the Alps were covered in mighty glaciers. Why did the prehistoric Greeks practice the identical surveying skills in their mountainous land and over maritime distances of 300 kilometers? Why the planning games with geometry also on the remote British islands?

It is time to prick up our ears. Who is responsible for the geometric grid over our countries? Who surveyed the earth millennia ago? That even includes a survey of Antarctica. We know about it from the charts of the

Turkish admiral Piri Reis. In 1513, he had created a new chart from more ancient ones he had found in Alexandria, and the coastline of Antarctica has clearly been included on it, including all the offshore islands. An Antarctic, remember, which did not exist at the time of Piri Reis because Antarctica, still covered in ice today, was unknown in 1513. (There is a more detailed explanation in *Im Namen von Zeus*.[29])

I am aware that this whole business of incomprehensible geometric facts is wearing on the nerves. It sounds somehow exotic, far-fetched; our reason refuses to accept what is clearly there. Our thinking shuts down in the face of the prehistoric land survey. We know that there was never a "megalithic people," that a "worldwide kingdom" never existed, that our "Stone Agers" did not maintain contact with one another over thousands of kilometers, that there were no global means of transport. And yet these facts undeniably lie right in front of our eyes. In order to come to grips with this incredible reality, we first have to jettison all preconceptions, be they from politics, religion, or science. Our scientific thinking keeps to scientific rules that the British statesman Sir Francis Bacon (1561–1626) formulated almost 400 years ago. Francis Bacon was a controversial and combative figure. He was considered conceited, well-read, boundlessly ambitious, and, for good measure, devoid of feelings. He was—rightly—annoyed by the unscientific attitudes and superstitions of his time. Hence in his work *Novum Organum*, he demanded experiments that could be replicated at any time. Knowledge was a way to achieve power, for Francis Bacon. ("Knowledge is power.") On the path to knowledge, all illusions (so-called idols) had to be avoided. The whole of science still keeps to this maxim today. It has brought us magnificent results, but at the same time ensured that numerous subject have never been tackled at all.

Then, in 1975, philosopher of science Professor Paul Feyerabend, who taught at the University of California, Berkeley, for a long time, published his "anything goes" approach.[30] His hypothesis contradicted the idea of a continuous process of finding scientific truth as had been demanded by Francis Bacon. Feyerabend postulated that a scientific method could only produce the result permitted by that method. In fact, many scientific innovations occurred precisely through *not* observing methodological rules but by breaking them. We need both: Francis Bacon and Paul Feyerabend.

The fact that huge swathes of land were surveyed in prehistoric times calls for the thinking of a Paul Feyerabend. Our logic continues to be puny;

83

we do not dare to lift our gaze beyond our own navels. We are basically in the process of waking up and are laboriously keeping our eyes shut. It is high time to investigate the motives that lie behind the surveyed facts of our prehistory. And to do so without any restrictions. "Anything goes!"[31]

Who did the survey work millennia ago? Why? By what means? Here are a bunch of off-the-cuff thoughts:

- Feng shui, the Chinese teaching of magnetic fields?
- Electrostatic fields?
- Magnetism?
- Infrared? Ultrasound?
- Microwaves?
- Cosmic radiation?
- Ant or termite mounds?
- Geomancy?
- Old paths?
- Mineral or water veins?

- Border markings?
- Gaia? (The earth as a living being, wherein the lines are its veins.)[32]
- A grid to control and influence human beings?

Nothing seems to fit. The magnetic fields of feng shui do not just run in straight and rectangular lines, but also in curves. The same applies to mineral and water veins and all the other types of field. Border markings across thousands of kilometers and across the sea do not fit with the "Stone Agers." They would, in any case, have run their borders along water courses. Ants and termites do not build their nests along straight lines either. Now it is undisputed that the survey points in Greece are definitively older than Euclid and Plato. The "Stone Agers" which we learned about in school are ruled out in any case. They simply were not globally active.

Perplexity is the word for "bewildered," "poleaxed." Perplexity sets in when thinking has reached a dead end. What are we to do? What happens next? Who, for heaven's sake, surveyed ancient Greece x-thousand years ago? Negating facts is unscientific in the profoundest sense of the word.

Plato expressly notes in his book *Timaeus* (Chapters 7 and 8) that these geometric relationships were based on accounts several thousands of years old. From whom? The ancient Chinese report that at the time of the Emperor Fuk Hi "a monster with the body of a horse and the head of a dragon" had appeared out of the waters of the Meng Ho River.[33] The speaking monster carried large diagrams of the cosmos and the earth on its back. Something similar is reported by the Babylonian priest Berossus (c. 350 BC) in his *Babylonica*. A being called "Oannes" had risen from the waters of the Erythraean Sea (today known as the Arabian Sea) and had instructed human beings in all things, including how to survey land. The same teacher is called Yma in the holy book of the Parsees, the *Avesta*.[34] Even the God of the Old Testament explains to the patient prophet Job, "Where wast thou when I laid the foundations of the earth?...Who has laid the measures thereof?...Who hath stretched the line upon it?" (Job 38: 4–5)

We people of today survey the earth for quite practical purposes. How far is point A from point B? How long does it take to get there? Air routes would be impossible without a global system of coordinates. Were there flyers in antiquity, far superior to the ordinary people? A stupid idea? Almost 30 years ago, Dr. Dileep Kumar Kanjilal, professor at the Sanskrit College in Calcutta, underpinned precisely this hypothesis with a thorough analysis.[35] (I was permitted to reproduce a section of his work on flying machines in ancient India in a previous book.[36]) Kanjilal provides evidence for everything he writes from the correct sources. It can be checked by every expert. A short extract follows:

> The *Rigveda* contains well-known hymns which are addressed to the divine "Ashvin" twins, the "Rbhus," and other gods. These hymns contain the first indications of vehicles which were capable of flying through the air with living beings on board. These flying vehicles are described in the *Rigveda* as "Rathas." The word can be translated analogously as "vehicles" or "chariots." The "Rbhus" built a flying chariot for the "Ashvin" twins who were considered to be the physicians among the gods. This flying chariot was extremely comfortable. It was possible to fly everywhere with it, even above the highest cloud layers and into the "heavens" (firmament). The hymns mention that this flying chariot was faster than thought. At least three persons were required to operate it.... The heavenly war chariot as described was fuelled with liquids which cannot be correctly translated today. The words "madhu" and "anna" come closest in meaning to "honey" and "liquid." The chariot moved through the sky with greater ease than a bird, swept up toward the sun and even as far as the moon, and landed on earth with a great noise... When the vehicle came down from the clouds great crowds gathered on the ground to watch the landing....[37]

Without precise maps, the pilots of such flying machines would not have known where on earth their favorites or their enemies were located. Even the legendary King Solomon possessed a "chariot which traveled through the air and which he had made in accordance with the wisdom lent him by God."[38] If we read the most ancient Ethiopian account, the *Kebra Nagast*, then Solomon "covered a distance of three months in one day on his flying machine, without sickness and suffering, without hunger and thirst, without sweat and exhaustion."[39] Hardly surprising that such a skilled pilot had to possess excellent aerial charts. Arabia's most important geographer and encyclopaedist, Al-Mas'udi (895–956) wrote in his *Histories* that Solomon had owned maps which showed "the heavenly bodies, the stars, the earth with its continents and oceans, the inhabited regions, its plants and animals and many other amazing things."[40]

The finding that at least large parts of our earth had already been surveyed in prehistoric times is clearly verifiable. By *whom*? *Why*? Nowadays we not only survey the whole planet with satellites, determine the heights of mountains and depths of the oceans, but small surfaces such as a finger tip or face can also be registered. A grid made up of squares is laid over the face despite the irregularities of nose and eyes. They can be enlarged or reduced, and every detail in the corresponding square can be called up. Reassembled, we have the whole face again. Aldous Huxley's *Brave New World*[41] has become reality thanks to this technology of grid squares. Surveillance cameras observe crowds in railway stations, streets, stadiums, or at passport control. Every face is recorded by the camera and disassembled into small squares by a computer in seconds. If all the details fit with the image of a wanted person, there is a direct hit. The authorities now know the location of the person concerned.

The things we can do today, the things we will be able to do the day after tomorrow, was already old hat for the gods millennia ago. They operated Aldous Huxley's surveillance system to perfection. Precise maps were essential when they flew on earth—and grid squares for keeping an eye on their creatures. I suspect the system is still working today. As recently as 25 years ago, the radio astronomer Professor Ronald Bracewell of Stanford University, developed his hypothesis of "super galactic communities." This club only admits mature societies; all the others are monitored.[42] And his colleague, Professor James Deardorff, went one disturbing step further with his "zoo hypothesis."[43] According to this idea, the earth is viewed by the extraterrestrials as a refuge, a kind of "zoological garden." The prerequisite for the proper working of a zoo is the goodwill of the keepers and the zoo visitors. Thus visitors are prohibited from destroying the nesting sites of rare birds, feeding live dogs to crocodiles, provoking lions, or stealing poisonous snakes. All the visitors to the zoo must observe the rules. The animals are exclusively for looking at and, for the study of their development. The keepers for their part maintain a very close watch that the rules are observed and they know, of course, which species among the animals possesses greater intelligence than the rest: human beings. The keepers also know that it is only a matter of time before human beings have developed the technologies to break out of their zoo. Should they be allowed to do that? Are human beings perhaps a danger to keepers and zoo visitors? Is humanity being monitored, from millennia ago to the present day?

This thought might appear totally fanciful at first sight. We, the crowning glory of creation, the apex of evolution, nothing more than the most advanced apes in a global zoo? It is worth considering something which appears as completely ridiculous as that, as the following example shows.

On March 24, 1967, First Lieutenant Robert Salas of the U.S. Air Force was on duty at Malmstrom Air Force Base in Montana. A message came through that an elliptical, red object was hovering over the Oscar Flight control center. The Oscar Flight control center is not any old Air Force base, but a top-secret site because that is where intercontinental missiles mounted with nuclear warheads are kept in underground silos. While First Lieutenant Salas phoned the base commander, "the warning lights for the missiles went out one after the other on the status console, which meant that the missiles were deactivated."[44] Not a single missile could be started any longer; all had dropped off. And this happened while the missiles were 18 meters underground in their silos, and each missile was 1.5 kilometers away from the next one. Moreover, each silo had its own independent power supply and control and switching circuits. The same thing had already happened a week previously on the morning of March 16, 1967, at the Echo Flight base 45 kilometers away. A total of 20 intercontinental missiles had been immobilized.

These and similar cases are reported by the science journalist Leslie Kean in her recent book *UFOs: Generals, Pilots and Government Officials Break Their Silence.*[45] But is it not precisely the large nations that have closed their UFO offices? Is it not the Americans and British who no longer want to spend money on the registration of stupid, useless UFO documents? Correct! The real reason for this action is not, however, the reason which the public is fed. It is not about a lack of credibility among the witnesses, not about the lack of interest in the media, not about the unscientific nature of the whole subject, not about the validity of the documentation, including numerous film and radar documents. It is, plain and simple, the recognition that we human beings cannot do anything about it; an admission of our total impotence with regard to the UFO phenomenon. What is there to tell the public? You are all under surveillance? We are the inhabitants of a global zoo and totally impotent against our keepers?

There is even a positive side to the whole shebang. The superpowers would not have been able to destroy our refuge or pollute it with nuclear contamination. The keepers would have prevented it.

Grid squares or sectors would be very sensible for the total automatic monitoring of the zoo. A diagonal line drawn through a square turns it into two triangles. What did Horus, the divine son of Osiris and Isis say? The eye of Horus keeps watch. In modern times: God sees all. Whoever God might be.

FALSE DOCTRINES

Abydos lies 561 kilometers south of Cairo, directly on the Nile. The Egyptians of the Old Kingdom (2600–2200 BC) were already doing archaeology there: "They turned over the ground."[1] What they were looking for at that time is just as unknown as the origins of Abydos. Today it is the temples of Sethos I (1294–1279 BC) and his son Ramses II (1279–1213 BC) that dominate the scene. **(Images 86–87)** But the temple complex of Sethos I partially rests on foundations from those mythical times of which we know nothing. Directly behind the temple there is the so-called Osireion, a complex constructed from giant granite blocks which, looked at from a technological perspective, does not fit in with the Sethos temple, whichever way you look at it.

As long ago as 1726, when no official department of archaeology yet existed, the Frenchman Granger (real name Tourtechot) started digging in Abydos. At that time, the whole complex lay under the desert sands and only a few upright columns signaled a structure under the surface. The next Frenchman to burrow in Abydos, Emile Amélineau, discovered tombs from the First and Second Dynasty, about 5,000 years in the past when calculated from today. In 1859, when Abydos had been buried by the desert again, Auguste Mariette, the subsequent founder of the Egyptian Museum in Cairo, had Abydos shoveled free again. Eventually the Britons Sir Flinders Petrie and Margaret Murray undertook research in Abydos in 1903, and in 1912, the famous Swiss Egyptologist Professor Edouard

111

86

Naville (1844–1926) discovered a granite stone gateway in the ground with various subterranean chambers. Naville investigated the up to 100-tonne granite blocks of the Osireion and finally concluded with resignation that this complex had to be considered as the "oldest structure in the whole of Egypt."[2] **(Images 88–91)**

The Osireion lies 15 meters below the level of the temple of Sethos I and consists of massive granite blocks without any ornamentation—comparable with the megaliths of Stonehenge in southern England. Why is the complex called "Osireion"? Because according to legend, the head of the heavenly god Osiris is said to be hidden there. Osiris is equivalent to Orion. He originally came from that constellation. He studied humans, taught them, and was—similar to the Greek Apollo and Peruvian Viracocha—a helpful god. It was Osiris who traveled throughout the world and taught human beings agriculture, respect for one another, and, particularly, the magic power of music and song. But Osiris had a jealous brother, Seth. He wanted the earth and all its people for himself, and so he treacherously murdered his brother, Osiris. In order to prevent him ever coming back to life, Seth cut up the body of Osiris into 14 pieces and buried the different parts of the body in different places—the backbone in Busiris, a leg in Philae, the phallus in Mendes, and the most important part of the body, the head, in Abydos—hence "the Osireion." The head of the god Osiris has not been found in Abydos to the present day. And that is unlikely to change, because Osiris, like his mystical companions, belongs to the clan of the extraterrestrials. They are reported about in the so-called Pyramid Texts from the Fifth and Sixth Dynasty, whereby it remains an open question how long the texts were already in existence before someone chiselled them into the granite. These texts are full of gods who descend to earth from the heavens, and of pharaohs who were accorded the honor of visiting the world of the gods. As the confused spirit of our times only sees abstract thinking behind the Pyramid Texts, our gullible academics from the last century conjured wishful thinking and dreams of the priests into these texts or the journey of the pharaoh after death.

The Pyramid Text of Pepi I equates Osiris with the constellation of Orion: "See, Osiris comes as Orion, heaven has conceived you in Orion, you were born with Orion...."[3] In the Pyramid Texts of Unas (2356–2323 BC) also, Osiris journeys to the "heavenly way."[4] **(Images 92–97)** He is, like Horus, an "inhabitant of the horizon" who "pushes off from the earth" in his vessel, who (in verse 303) "ascends to heaven."[5] Osiris originally clearly lives in fateful heaven—but heaven is not the place of blessedness after death. The term "heaven" refers to space. I recommend that our hard-working Egyptologists, who are all sincerely translating Pyramid Texts, read the "Utterances" (verses) with modern glasses. The modern interpretation makes sense, as the following examples show:

> "Heaven trembles, the earth shakes before me, I possess magic powers. I have come to worship Orion..." (Utt. 472)

> "A stairway to heaven has been set up for me so that I can ascend to heaven and I climbed up on the smoke of the large vessel... and thundered beyond heaven in your barque. I am permitted to lift off the land in your barque..." (Utt 267)

> "The doors of the (?) which are in the firmament were opened for me, the metal doors which are in starry heaven lie open for me..." (Utt. 584)

> "The prince descends from the inner horizon in a great storm..." (Utt. 669)[6]

88

89

90

91

92

93

94

95

96

97

And so on. Heavenly doors are open, gods descend in smoke and fumes, pharaohs are allowed to fly along, there is thunder and noise on earth, the sand swirls up and the perpetrators of the spectacle are always the gods, be it in ancient India, Tibet, Japan, in the Bible (Ezekiel), or elsewhere. Now we must not, the Egyptologists always tell us, compare such texts with any kind of reality. The pharaoh's journey to heaven after death is what is always meant. An honourable view—based on the hard work of prestigious Egyptologists—and yet a misunderstanding on a grand scale.

Egypt, with all its original gods of Ra, Osiris, Isis, Horus, and so on, is connected with the myths of other civilisations. Different names, similar deeds. The same applies to the connection between Sumer and Egypt. In Sumerian cuneiform scripts, there is a long report from the princess and high priestess Enheduanna, called the Temple Hymns of Enheduanna. They were created about 4,300 years ago. The text has been translated by Sumerologists and made to fit a preconceived model, which is just as wrong as the Egyptian Pyramid Texts with the alleged journey to heaven of the pharaohs after death. The specialist Dr. Hermann Burgard, who studied Sumerology for decades, who can read cuneiform writing in the original and who knows the ancient texts and their interpreters, says that the Sumerologists are working "improperly and making untenable claims."[7] Dr. Burgard translated the Temple Hymns of Enheduanna[8] and reached the absolutely convincing conclusion that all previous translations of the Temple Hymns are based on erroneous assumptions which are no longer tenable. Millennia ago, the princess and high priestess Enheduanna did not report about some psychologically dressed-up circus of the gods, about underworlds and mythological drivel, but about very real technical things, such as:

- Ramps for flying machines.
- Production of fuel.
- Storage rooms for fuel.
- Terrible explosions in which hundreds of people died.
- Flying machines rising into the heavens.
- Spaceships in orbit.
- Radio traffic.
- Refinement of scrap metals.
- Metal alloys for flying machines.

98

Dr. Herman Burgard's work is the milestone, the breakthrough on the way to an appropriate contemporary translation. This is not some amateur spinning a yarn. Enheduanna's Temple Hymns are analyzed by an expert who criticises the Sumerologists for "sloppy writing or centuries of misunderstanding."[9]

I know of new translations from India[10] in which professors dared to clear up the old misconceptions with thorough specialist knowledge. Dr. Hermann Burgard's translation of the Temple Hymns of Enheduanna is just as much of a serious work, a textbook based on sound knowledge. I can see light at the end of the tunnel.

That Sethos I built the Osireion in Abydos is as likely as the moon being made of cheese. Here—as in Pumapunku in the highlands of Bolivia—"gods" were at work. The specialists think that Sethos I had mighty blocks transported from Aswan to Abydos. The two locations are separated by about 400 kilometers of Nile, including rapids. (Today there are locks for the shipping.) Aswan granite is the hardest in the world. The heavy blocks, up to 100 tonnes in weight, would have had to be polished at their destination. Before that, the ancient engineers would have

99

fitted the monoliths with recesses and notches in specific places so that the upper and lower blocks could be precisely fitted into one another. **(Images 98–99)**

Irritatingly, the building site was lower than the level of the Nile. Why that had to be is a secret of the gods. So high-tech methods were used to prevent the waters of the Nile from flooding the building site. The columns, which supported the whole thing, could not just be punched into the soft substrate. So a foundation made of megalithic slabs had to be provided, with notches to precisely position the heavy blocks. **(Images 100–101)** Once they were securely in place, this was followed by the absolute master stroke of the prehistoric planners. Monster cranes, like those in the impressive 3D film *Avatar*, were brought up, which lowered the massive crossbeams with meticulous precision onto the granite columns. And it was done so that every notch fit exactly with its counterpart.

None of the Egyptologists who propagate such pseudo solutions appear to have the faintest knowledge of engineering. Let us just remember the evolution of technology. Nothing simply exists. Everything has to be thought out, invented, planned, developed, built, and, finally, transported.

100

101

102

103

Where—so help us Osiris!—are the actual workshops for the technologies which were used, where the developmental history of the stone cutters, ropes, lifting platforms, rope winches, rollers, and so on? The ancient Egyptians had hemp ropes, the experts tell us. That material is suitable, at best, for a towing capacity of 3 tonnes. But in Abydos, crossbeams weighing 30 tonnes were used. (**Images 102–104**) How many ropes would be required for loads like that? When does the pulling rope jump off the shaft? When do the bars on the capstans splinter? When does a lifting platform collapse and chip the edges of the monoliths already cleanly fitted below it? The monoliths of the Osireion of Abydos do not have a scratch. The workmen on the Osireion did not permit themselves a single error.

All unnecessary, the experts reply, and point to the tomb of the Overlord Djehutihotep (c. 1870 BC). A picture on a wall there shows 170 men dragging a statue through the desert with ropes. And a tomb from the time of Amenemhet I (1991–1962 BC) even mentions ropes. There are even images of pulleys from the Eighteenth Dynasty. But between the Abydos of the god Osiris (or the builders of the Great Pyramid) and the Eighteenth Dynasty there are about 600 years. If the technology of the Eighteenth Dynasty had been used in Abydos (and in the Great Pyramid), it would mean that the Egyptians had learnt nothing in a 600-year period. And the technology of the Eighteenth Dynasty was useless for the crossbeams of the Osireion in any case—too primitive for the precise cutting, too difficult for the crossbeams. Now the temple of Sethos I lies *above* the Osireion. So the Osireion must have been standing before Sethos was able to build his temple walls—walls, incidentally, in which smaller stones were layered on top of one another. One does not have to be a genius to see it: the *oldest* technology of the Osireion, which lies under the Sethos temple, is mightier, more perfect, and more grandiose than the temple lying above it. According to the evolution of technology, it should be precisely the other way round. In the learning process, we start on a small scale; the monumental comes later as technology develops.

What was this Osireion for, in any case? It was allegedly a cenotaph (pseudo tomb) for the god Osiris. Can the perspective get any narrower?

We are too quickly satisfied with the first answer. Our knowledge is dripping with complacency—because "we know it all." The results of the exact sciences can be tested at any time. But archaeology, which I greatly admire, is one of the information-gathering sciences. As such, it is open to reinterpretation at any time. Precise science is something different.

The Great Pyramid—all the experts agree on that—was built by Cheops (2551–2528 BC). He belonged to the Fourth Dynasty. **(Image 105–111)** Is there anyone who bothers to query that in the 80 years in which the Fourth Dynasty ruled, about 9,000,000 cubic meters of building volume was handled? That is for the pyramids of Sneferu (2575–2551 BC), Cheops (2551–2528 BC), Djedefre (2528–2520 BC), and Chefren (2520–2494 BC). In these 80 years—the experts believe—12,066,000 stone blocks were quarried out of the rock, cut, polished, measured, transported, and inserted into the structure in the right place. It gets even better. The excavation and leveling work, the manufacture and repair of tools, the incredibly elaborate ramps and scaffolding, are not included in the more than 12 million blocks. The whole of lower Egypt must have been a big building site, not to mention the material requirements and the provisions for the masses of people. And the most absurd thing of all: neither the team of designers nor the architects, nor a foreman, priest, or pharaoh wasted any words on mentioning the building work. The Egyptologist Dr. Eva Eggebrecht writes in this respect: "The contemporary silence about the construction of the pyramids becomes incomprehensible if we recall that the necropolises were not deathly silent cities of secrecy.... Sacrifices were made, priests came and went.... None of them left as much as a note which would answer even a single question about the construction of the pyramids."[11]

But what if everything were quite different? If the men of the Fourth Dynasty were unable to say anything about the structures because there was nothing to say? Were the buildings already dotted around in the landscape when the Fourth Dynasty began to rule?

It is likely that more than 1,000 volumes have been written about the Great Pyramid. At least once a year, a manuscript lands on my desk, and each author is convinced of having definitively cracked the "pyramid nut." God knows these are not cranks but down-to-earth, hard-working people, in many cases engineers who are familiar with construction and surveying. Often they have sat at their calculations and comparisons for years, experimented and, of course, deployed computers. And yet each one of these upright pyramid crackers comes to a different result. And none of them understand why their competitors do not reach the same conclusions as themselves. A different logic rules in each brain. Now I am neither an engineer nor a stone mason, and

109

110

112

therefore do not even start to grapple with the phenomenon of the technology which was used to build the pyramids. As a lateral thinker and someone who knows classical literature, other inconsistencies and contradictions catch my eye which simply cannot be ignored. Let me start with the Grand Gallery in the Cheops pyramid.

The Grand Gallery is a miracle of construction which is difficult to digest. It is an extended space which is about 47 meters long and 8.5 meters high, running upwards at an angle to the so-called King's Chamber. **(Image 112)** The granite beams opposite one another do not lie horizontally. No, like an extra slap in the face for us clever clogs, the monoliths slope upward at the same inclination as the Grand Gallery. The beams and slabs have been worked with such precision that it is difficult to see any joints. **(Image 113)** The architects of the Cheops pyramid planned and created this miracle—so we are told. But something is not quite right here.

113

114

115

116

117

118

119

Cheops' father was called Sneferu and was presumably older than his son. This Pharaoh Sneferu (2575–2551 BC) had a pyramid built in Dahshur, among other things. From the outside, it looks like a pile of boulders—as if the structure had stood in the water for decades. **(Image 114)** What is inside this mountain of rubble? A "Grand Gallery," with granite blocks arranged on top of one another, like that of his son Cheops. Here there is not enough space for a razor blade between the stone beams either. Every cut is perfectly. **(Images 115–116)** For heaven's sake—Sneferu preceded Cheops straight out of the Stone Age. But his builders displayed a "Grand Gallery" before Cheops. From what magic workshop did the knowledge, the planning, the technology used by the Stone Age person Sneferu come? Where, pray tell, is the developmental history of the technology when the father of Cheops was already practicing what his son's architects were allegedly the first to develop?

Anyone who, dripping with sweat, today climbs into the Great Pyramid first enters a passageway reminiscent of a Swiss mineshaft. The hole was made in the year AD 827. At the time, the Caliph Abdullah Al-Mamun wanted to get at the treasures which he assumed to be inside the pyramid. His raiding party did not find any entrance, so the men

120

121

123

laboriously chiseled a shaft through the blocks of the pyramid. **(Images 117–118)** After 10 meters, the air became thin, stifling, and poisonous, because the torches used up what little oxygen there was. Unnerved, the troop wanted to give up, when suddenly they stood rooted to the spot. For a dull rolling sound and then a loud bang could be heard inside. Some stone must have dislodged and rumbled down. So the men tenaciously continued with their chiselling and finally came upon a passageway. That led to the actual entrance 16.5 meters above the ground or 10 layers of stone higher than the hole made by Al-Mamun. **(Image 119)** In the opposite direction, the shaft led to a corridor which is described as an "ascending passageway." Boards with chicken ladders were put on the ground for the tourists, and railings were fixed to the walls. **(Images 120–122)** Anyone who wants to go up the passageway must crouch, because the 23-meter-long section is only about 1 meter high. Then the tourist—panting and dripping with sweat—enters the Grand Gallery. And that is when the next justified questions present themselves.

The ascending passageway that leads to the Grand Gallery is so small and low that not even the sarcophagus which stands in the King's Chamber would fit through it. **(Image 123)** The experts say that we have to imagine the Grand Gallery as a long, ascending hall in which stately processions proceeded to pay their last respects to the pharaoh. Yet the same procession of priests would first have had to crawl through the ascending passageway to reach the Grand Gallery at all. That does not make sense. Why this low ascending passageway?

At the upper end of the Grand Gallery we have the entrance to the King's Chamber. Three-tonne stone trapdoors once blocked the entrance. The King's Chamber feels like a cathedral. The rectangular space measures 5.22 meters in a north-south direction and 10.47 meters from east to west. The height is 5.82 meters. It is hard to understand why, with such dimensions, it is called a chamber. The walls consist of five granite beams laid one on top of the other—not set next to one another! The floor has also been lined with granite slabs. The walls feel like smooth marble. The ceiling of pink Aswan granite consists of nine huge beams and has been assembled with such precision that the joints are visible, at best, as thin black threads. And above this ceiling we have the next piece of nonsense: the relief chambers.

These are five hollow spaces stacked on top of one another above the King's Chamber. The pharaoh's engineers allegedly planned these five hollow spaces as relief chambers, the scientific consensus says. **(Image 124)** As long as 60 years ago, the Egyptologist Dr. Hermann Kees pointed out, "...the relief chambers over the coffin chamber of the Cheops pyramid, *which by the way serve no purpose in terms of statics,* are very original"[12] (emphasis by Erich von Däniken). Who, then, had the unfortunate idea of calling these hollow spaces "relief chambers," and why do hordes of scribblers and archaeologists quote this rubbish? The relief chambers do not even lie on the axis of the pyramid (that is, under its point), and they relieve nothing whatsoever. Furthermore, intentionally planned relief chambers assume that the Cheops engineers of 5,000 years ago had calculated the total weight of the pyramid. How can that be reconciled with the knowledge of the time? Such calculations have only become possible today as a result of computers. Would the King's Chamber have collapsed without relief chambers? Would the pyramid have caved in? Nonsense. The space above the ceiling could simply have been supported

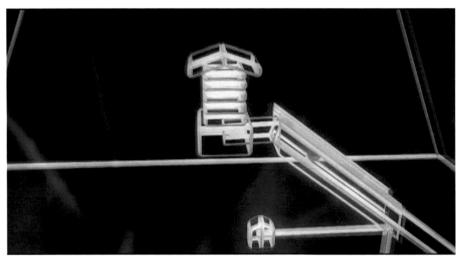

124

with granite beams whose weight did not rest on the ceiling of the King's Chamber. Moreover, where are the other relief chambers in the pyramid? The relief chambers spontaneously remind me of a Shinto temple—a gate to another world.

The experts provide evidence of the fact that Cheops from the Fourth Dynasty built the pyramid, evidence which, on closer inspection, turns out to be of little value, as I intend to show. What do the ancient historians actually have to say about it, those men who wrote about Egypt, about the construction of the pyramids, some 2,000 years ago?

Diodorus of Sicily (first century BC), the author, no less, of a 40-volume work of history, states:

> The eighth king was Chemmis from Memphis. The latter governed for 50 years and built the largest of the three pyramids which are considered to belong to the seven Wonders of the World.... It consists completely of hard stone, which is very difficult to work but also lasts eternally.... It is told that the stone was brought from far away in Arabia.... And the most wondrous thing is, although works of such magnitude were built here, and the surrounding region consists of nothing but sand, no trace has been left either of an embankment or the cutting of stones so that the impression is given

as if this work had not been created gradually by human hand but had been placed finished all at once into the sandy desert as if by a god....[13]

The greatest mocker among the classical historians, Gaius Plinius Secundus, who moreover had the advantage of knowing all the works of his predecessors, also described the Egyptian pyramids:

The material for the largest pyramids was supplied by the quarries of Arabia and...all three (pyramids) were completed in 78 years and four months. The following authors have described the pyramids: Herodotus, Euhemerus, Duris of Samos, Aristagoras, Dionysius, Artemidorus, Alexander Polyhistor, Butoridas, Antisthenes, Demetrius, Demoteles, and Apion. But none of them can say who actually built them....[14]

Not bad. Gaius knows 12 works on the pyramids and expressly notes that no one knows who built them. And that millennia ago.

In 1850, a stele was found in the ruins of the Isis temple which today can be seen in the Egyptian Museum in Cairo. The inscription says that Cheops had established the house of Isis, the lady of the pyramid, beside the house of the Sphinx. If Isis is described as "lady of the pyramid," then the Great Pyramid was already standing when Cheops appeared on the scene. Furthermore, the Sphinx **(Images 125–126)** would also already have existed which, in the opinion of the archaeologists, is only said to have been built by Chefren, who succeeded Cheops.

In around AD 1360, the Arab historian Al-Maqrizi (1364–1442) collected all the available documents about the pyramids. He published that material in the "pyramid chapter" of his work *Hitat*.[15] In it, we learn that the Great Pyramid was built as long ago as before the Flood by a king named Saurid. Who was this Saurid? The *Hitat* says about him that "he was Hermes, whom the Arabs call Idris."[16] God himself had instructed him in astronomy and revealed to him that a catastrophe would come to pass over the earth, but that a small part of it would remain in which the sciences would be urgently required. Thereupon "Saurid" alias Hermes alias Idris had built the pyramids. This is explained in greater detail in Chapter 33 of the *Hitat*:

The first Hermes, who was called the Thrice-Great in his capacity as prophet, king, and sage. He is the one whom the Hebrews call Enoch, the son of Jared, son of Mahalalel, son of Kenan, son of Enos, son of Seth, son of Adam—blessings be upon him—and who read in the stars that the Flood would come. So he had the pyramids built and saved in them treasures, learned writings, and everything about which he was concerned that it would be lost and could disappear, in order to protect these things and keep them well.[17]

It is not only in the *Hitat* that Enoch alias Hermes is named as the builder of the pyramids. The Arab explorer and writer Ibn Battuta (14th century) also affirmed that Enoch had built the pyramids before the Flood "to keep in them books of science and knowledge and other valuable objects."[18]

Confusing. But nothing was found in the pyramids. Not so fast! The discoveries are still to be made.

The *Hitat* counts six generations *before* Enoch. Al-Maqrizi, the author, clearly knows what he is talking about, because Enoch is the seventh patriarch before the Flood. Enoch means "the initiate, the insightful, the knowledgeable" in Hebrew. I have reported about this Enoch in many of my books and will therefore refrain from any repetition here. (The most detailed report about Enoch can be found in source *Falsch Informiert.*[19])

On the Sumerian King List <WB444>, an engraved stone block which can be admired in the British Museum, 10 primal kings ruled from the creation of the earth to the Flood. **(Image 127)** The seventh on this list from before the Flood is said to have lived in the sun city of Sippar. The gods themselves had instructed him "in the art of writing and seeing into the future."[20] According to Genesis, this is Enoch. The fame of this seventh ruler from before the Flood was so great that the Babylonian King Nebuchadnezzar I, who lived much later in about 1100 BC, traced his lineage back to this pre-Flood king. Cuneiform translations in recent decades have revealed that it is precisely this seventh ruler who "ascended to the heavens." Just like Enoch. It also fits in with his own description of the extraterrestrials, the so-called heavenly guardians. They teach him their language, dictate scientific books to him and finally take him with them on their journey into the space. All of it in detail and told personally by Enoch in the first person.[21]

128

But it was Cheops and not Enoch who built the Great Pyramid, the critics reply. This Cheops does indeed occur in the lists of kings, for example on a temple wall in Abydos. There we have the Cheops from the Fourth Dynasty—but not a single glyph mentions that he is the builder of the Great Pyramid. Why ever not? Because the ancient Egyptians did not know who had the pyramid built. And what about the glyph and the name "Cheops" daubed into one of the relief chambers?

The chemist and pyramid researcher Alireza Zarei refers in his exceptionally well-documented book *Die verletzte Pyramide* (*The Damaged Pyramid*) to various ways of writing and interpretations of the name "Cheops." There is little which is unambiguous and clear. Moreover, so Alireza Zarei writes, "a further inscription of the Pharaoh Cheops" had been found "on the fourth layer of stones of the west wall."[22] Finally, a 5-centimeter-high image of a seated Cheops had turned up in the Chontamenti temple in Abydos. It can be admired today in the Egyptian Museum. **(Image 128)** Yet not a whisper here either that the seated

129

Cheops had ordered the Great Pyramid to be built. And to dot the "i," the father of history, Herodotus, names Cheops/Khufu as the builder of the pyramid. What more does anyone want? Cheops has been nailed down. Or has he?

The detective work is not as simple as it looks. To begin with, it must be noted that none of the historians of antiquity who visited Egypt 2,000 years ago and asked the priests at the time know anything about a Cheops. The exception is Herodotus: he came from Halicarnassus in Asia Minor and became the globetrotter of his age. Egypt, which he entered in July 448 BC, was a new world for Herodotus. Thus he took a note of everything that his interlocutors told him about the history of their country and meticulously distinguished between what he was told and what he saw with his own eyes. Herodotus wrote *he had been told* a Pharaoh called "Khufu" had had the Great Pyramid built within 20 years. "Khufu" is Egyptian—in Greek he is called "Cheops," hence the name Cheops. In this case, Egyptologists ignored all other historians who knew nothing about a Cheops and threw

130

131

132

themselves on Herodotus' statement. The following example shows the selective way in which they proceeded.

Herodotus reports that a pharaoh called Menes had ordered the Nile to be diverted above Memphis. The Egyptologists like this statement. Eighteen lines later, the same Herodotus writes, "Menes was followed by 330 kings whose names the priests read out from a book." The diversion of the Nile fit, the 330 kings did not. Or, in the second book of his *Histories*, Herodotus writes that the priests in Thebes had personally shown him 341 statues and all these statues together represented 11,340 years. At that time, the gods had still lived among humans. Since then, they had no longer come. Herodotus gives the express assurance: "The Egyptians are absolutely sure of that, because they have continuously counted and written down the years."[23]

For Egyptology, the 333 kings or 11,340 years are absolute nonsense, even if all the other historians of antiquity provide equally "impossible" numbers of years—numbers which, without exception, go beyond 10,000 BC.

133

Cheops is said to have been a tyrant. Vanity lies in the nature of every tyrant. Yet the Great Pyramid of the Pharaoh Cheops is totally anonymous. How can a tyrant have the mightiest structure on earth built without boasting about it, without immortalizing his name with just a single tiny glyph? The total absence of any inscription is nothing but perverse; the anonymity of the structure does not fit with the character of the principal.

Pliny wrote, "...so the creators of this vanity have rightly fallen victim to the past."[24] Vanity and namelessness are incompatible. If the Pharaoh Cheops was vain, indeed, a tyrant and oppressor (Herodotus), then his heroic deeds should be heralded on every wall. The objection has been raised that his oppressed people chiselled away the hieroglyphs praising the deeds of their dictator. When? The pyramid was completely sealed. No raving madman could enter it to give vent to his fury on the inscriptions of the pharaoh. Modern academic opinion, moreover, holds that no slaves were employed in ancient Egypt.[25] The first person to break open the pyramid after millennia was the Caliph Al-Mamun. What did he actually find?

134

Al-Mamun opened the Great Pyramid. I visited its interior and saw a large vaulted chamber whose base formed a square while it was round above. In the middle there was a square well shaft with the depth of ten cubits. If one climbs down into it, one discovers on each of its four sides a gateway leading to a large room in which corpses lie: the sons of Adam....[26]

In the *Hitat*, we can also read that Al-Mamun found several corpses with strange armour inside the pyramid, as well as books in an unfamiliar writing. Excuse me? Al-Mamun and his scholars would undoubtedly have been able to read hieroglyphs from the time of Cheops.

In about 300 BC, a priest and historian called Manetho lived in Egypt. Eight works are attributed to him, including a book on the history of Egypt. Manetho's books have been lost, but the historian Julius Africanus (died c. 240 BC) and the Church Father Eusebius (died AD 339) recorded information from Manetho.[27, 28] He reports that the first ruler of Egypt was Hephaestus, who had also brought fire. He was followed by Chronos; Osiris; Typhon, brother of Osiris; then Horus, son of Osiris and Isis. "After the gods, the demigods reigned for 1,255 years. And again other kings ruled for 1,817 years. Then another thirty kings of Memphis, 1,790 years. And then ten kings of Thinis for 350 years. The reign of the demigods comprised 5,813 years..."[29]

The Church Father Eusebius attempted to interpret Manetho's numbers—and all of them, not just the ones listed here—as lunar years. But the lunar years calculated backwards in earth years still produced a figure beyond 14,000 BC.

Things become even more confusing: according to the Sumerian King List <WB444>, the 10 primal kings ruled from the creation of the earth to the Flood, a total of 456,000 years. After the Flood, the "kingship descended from heaven again." The 23 kings after the Flood together still managed a reign of 24,510 years, 3 months, and 3.5 days. A comparison of the Sumerian and Babylonian figures with figures from distant India reveal something highly puzzling: Buddhism works with *yugas* (epochs). The number 4,320,000 of the Maha Yuga (Great Epoch) is identical with the one of the third pre-Flood primal king En-men-lu-ana. He ruled 12 "sars," which is 43,200 years. Or the number 288,000 of the Deva Yuga corresponds to the number of the sixth primal king with the magnificent name En-sipad-zid-ana. He managed a good 8 *sars*, which is 28,800 years. In Greece, we find the oldest literary reference to a world age in the poet Heraclitus. He specifies the number 10,800,000 years. The same basic value corresponds to the second period of the Sumerian primal kings, namely 30 *sars* or 108,000 years. Here, the important thing is not the zeros but the numbers.

This numbers game has absolutely nothing to do with the Cheops of the Fourth Dynasty and yet it illustrates something which is common to everything. In time immemorial, there must have been an original teaching—the numbers cannot be explained in any other way. These mysterious origins must, of necessity, lie very far in the past. The history books would know about it otherwise.

The scribbles of the word "Cheops" in the Great Pyramid do not prove that he built it. **(Image 129)** Although it is said that Al-Mamun was the first to have broken into the pyramid after Cheops, tomb robbers have always tunneled into the structure. Assuming for a moment that the pyramid already stood at the time of Cheops, it cannot be excluded that someone

136

broke into it then and daubed all kinds of things on the walls and ceiling of the relief chambers with red paint. Perhaps also the word Cheops, with the red paint then dripping through the cracks. It is also conceivable that there were several "Cheopses" in the long course of Egyptian history. After all, there were also several Ramses and several Amenemhets. We need only think of the 333 kings mentioned by Herodotus or the list of Manetho. It is also conceivable that the tyrant Cheops from the Fourth Dynasty appropriated the building. In the controversy about who was responsible for building the pyramid, I would like to put forward another thought which argues against the Cheops from the Fourth Dynasty—an argument which it has only become possible to advance because of the most recent discoveries in the pyramid.

Anyone who pokes around on the pyramid plateau will notice layers of stone with various deposits on them. It is hard to avoid the impression that water must have stood here at some point. That relates to walls and rock sections which tourists never get to see, but also the ramps. It is

137

particularly visible in the Valley of the Crows below the pyramids, but also on the section up to the pyramid of Chefren. Water rings are also visible on the so-called fourth pyramid, which is not accessible for tourists. (**Images 130–147**) Now this land positively did not lie under water in the Fourth Dynasty—otherwise Cheops would not have been able to plant his building there at all. (Always assuming he did so.) "Land submerged" would, however, fit very well with Enoch; after all, he lived before the Flood. Irritatingly, the pyramid of Cheops' father, Sneferu, looks like a pile of rubble from the outside. The stones have been worn away by wind and sand over thousands of years, the experts assure us. But the wind blows more strongly from some directions than from others. The traces of the erosion should vary, depending on where on the pyramid it occurred. But they don't. (**Image 148**)

138

139

140

141

142

143

144

145

146

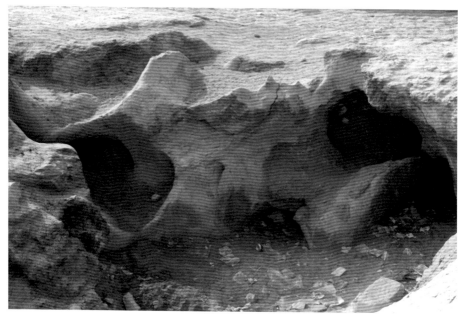

147

148

149

150

151

If the Cheops pyramid had been built *before* the Flood, it would have been submerged just like the (alleged) Sneferu pyramid. Where are the watermarks with Cheops? Salt crystals, for which there is no explanation, were found in some places inside the pyramid—for example, the ceiling of the "uppermost relief chamber is covered in incredibly large salt crystals."[30] The diligent Alireza Zarei has provided the photographic evidence. **(Image 149)** But if the Cheops pyramid had ever stood in water, should the traces of erosion not be visible just as much on the outside as with Sneferu's pyramid?

Consider this: Originally the Great Pyramid was covered with slabs. They were only broken off after Al-Mamun. These pyramid slabs—nicely cut to size—were used for parts of Cairo's city walls, mosques, and government buildings.

In the summer of 1986, the two French architects Jean-Patrice Dormion and Gilles Goidin discovered hollow spaces in the Cheops pyramid with their electronic detectors. With the assistance of the Ministry of State of Antiquities, microprobes were driven through stones 2.5 meters thick. Under the Queen's Chamber **(Images 150–151)**, the Frenchmen came upon a 3-meter-wide and 5.5-meter-high cavity filled with crystalline sand. What was the original purpose of this passageway?

Alerted by the success of the Frenchmen, the Japanese from Waseda University in Tokyo were not to be outdone. On January 22, 1987, a top team began its research into the Great Pyramid. Electronic measurements located various spaces and chambers inside the pyramid. The scientific report from Waseda University even refers to "a whole labyrinth" of passageways.[31]

In 1992, the geologist Dr. Robert M. Schoch from the College of General Studies of Boston University carried out geological measurements on the Sphinx together with Dr. Thomas L. Dobecki and other scientists. The result: the Sphinx is at least 5,000 years older than previously assumed.[32]

On March 22, 1993, at precisely 11:05 in the morning, the German engineer Rudolf Gantenbrink, with his robot "Upuaut," discovered a small door with two metal fittings inside the Great Pyramid. The discovery was made after a trip of about 60 meters, starting from the Queen's Chamber in an ascending direction inside the edifice. Gantenbrink's robot was a 6-kilogram tracked vehicle only 37 centimeters in length. This technical miracle was driven by seven independent electric motors. Two small

152

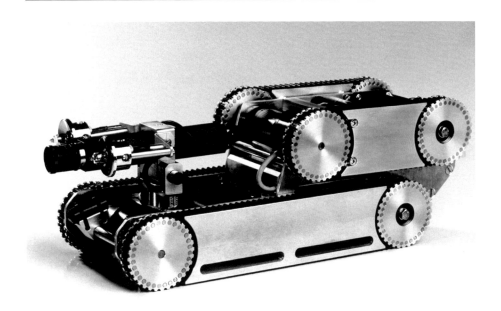

153

halogen spotlights and a swivelling and tilting Sony CCD mini video cam-era were attached to the front. **(Images 152–153)** The attempt was made at the time to deny Rudolf Gantenbrink's sensational discovery. People waffled about "soul shafts,"[33] "complete rubbish,"[34] and even a "delusion."[35] After its 60-meter trip, Rudolf Gantenbrink's robot had come to a halt in front of a small door. What lay behind that door? **(Image 154)**

A new robot, this one built by the National Geographic Society in the United States, drilled a hole through the little door. A camera was pushed through. It revealed another blocking stone, or little door, 20 centimeters further on.

Another robot, which the designers named "Djedi," with different abilities was required. A long arm was to reach through the hole created by National Geographic and drill through the "blocking stone" behind. On May 29, 2011 *Spiegel Online* reported: "A research robot has again driven into the mysterious shaft below the King's Chamber in the Cheops pyramid—but this time equipped with a swiveling camera."[36] **(Image 155)**

154

155

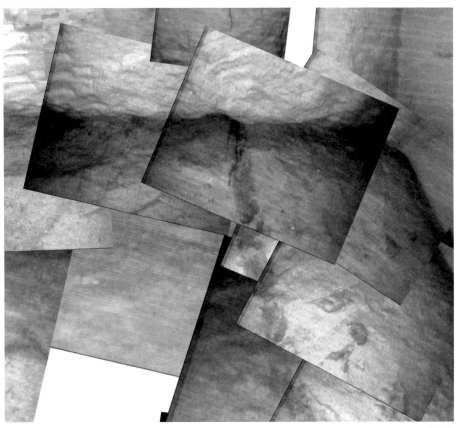

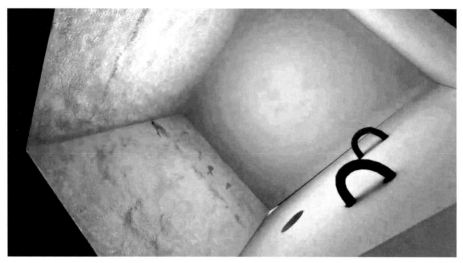

157

The magazine *Mysteries,* edited by the brilliant Swiss journalist Luc Bürgin, showed the pictures taken by the Djedi robot behind the blocking stone.[37] A new chamber with smoothly polished stones was visible. Illegible red markings, two handles clearly made of metal and a perfectly round hole could be seen on a side wall. **(Images 156-157)** And that makes it increasingly hard to relate the pyramid to the Cheops from the Fourth Dynasty. The planning of all the spaces, passageways, and chambers can no longer be reconciled with the brains of the people from the Iron and Bronze Age. So far we know about the following hollow spaces within the Cheops pyramid:

- The entrance, 16.5 meters above the ground with the descending passageway.
- The intersection of the descending passageway and ascending passageway and the shaft into the depths to the "unfinished tomb."
- The 119-meter-long shaft in the rock under the pyramid to the "unfinished tomb."
- The "unfinished tomb" at a depth of 35 meters under the pyramid, 14.02 meters long and 8.25 meters wide.
- The 3.5 meter vertical shaft from the "unfinished tomb" even deeper into the rock.
- The 23-meter-long ascending passageway.

- The 47-meter-long and 8.5-meter-high Grand Gallery.
- The five so-called relief chambers.
- The 38.15-meter-long horizontal passage to the inner King's Chamber.
- The 5.76-meter-long, 5.23-meter-wide, and 6.26-meter-high King's Chamber.
- The 6.85-meter-long passage to the King's Chamber.
- The 5.22-meter-wide, 10.47-meter-long, and 5.82-meter-high King's Chamber.
- The sand-filled hollow spaces under the horizontal passage to the inner King's Chamber (Dormion and Gilles).
- The 60-meter-long Gantenbrink shaft running upward at an angle from the King's Chamber.
- Its unexplored counterpart running upwards at the same angle from the north side of the King's Chamber.
- The newly discovered space behind the Gantenbrink shaft (Djedi).
- The shafts electronically located by the team from Waseda University, Tokyo.

If we do a rough calculation *just of the length* of the known shafts and spaces, and add the labyrinth of shafts and passageways located by the troupe from Waseda University, Tokyo, there should be about 1 kilometer of hollow space within the Great Pyramid. (**Image 158**) That does not take into account the volume (height, depth, and width) of the spaces. Impossible for the gents from the Bronze and Iron Age!

The Chefren pyramid is always excluded from this game. (**Image 159**) All the researchers throw themselves on Cheops, but Chefren also offers inexplicable phenomena. In the years 1968 and 1969 the Nobel Prize winner for physics, Dr. Louis Alvarez, undertook a radiation experiment in the Chefren pyramid. Alvarez and his team started from the known fact in physics that cosmic radiation bombards the earth around the clock. This radiation loses a fraction of its energy as it penetrates solid matter. Precise measurements can determine how many protons are not slowed down as much because they have passed through a hollow space. Using a spark chamber and an IBM computer, Alvarez measured the tracks of more than

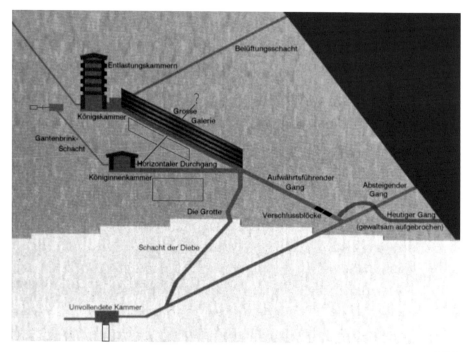

158

Translation of terms

Entlastungskammer—Discharge chamber

Belüftungsschacht—Air shaft

Königskammer—King's chamber

Königinnenkammer—Queen's chamber

Gantenbrinkschaft—Gantenbrink shaft

Horizontaler Durchgang—Horizontal passage

Die Grotte—The grotto

Schacht der Diebe—Thief's shaft

Unvollendete Grabkammer—Unfinished chamber

Grosse Gallerie—Grand gallery

Aufwährtsführender Gang—Ascending passageway passageway

Absteigender Gang—Descending passageway

Verschluss Blöcke—Closing blocks

Heutiger Eingang (gewaltsam aufgebrochen)—Today's entry (broken up violently)

159

2.5 million particles. Yet the oscillographs showed a chaotic pattern, just as if particles were arcing around a corner. The very expensive experiment, in which various American institutes, IBM, and Cairo's Ain Shams University participated, ended without a result. Dr. Amr Gohed, the head of archaeological research at the time, told journalists the findings were "scientifically impossible" and added that either "the structure of the pyramid is chaotic or there is a mystery which we cannot explain."[38]

Thus the curiosities are restricted not just to the Cheops pyramid; the Chefren pyramid also contains unsolved riddles. The chambers and passageways in the Chefren represent only a fraction of its interior life. (**Images 160-162**)

Back to the Cheops pyramid. It was not just a matter of piling one layer of stone on top of another and leaving a little gap here and there. Every single shaft, every passageway—just think of the 38-meter-long passage to the King's chamber or the 47-meter-long Grand Gallery—was part of an exact plan which existed from the start of construction. (**Image 163**) The

160

shaft under the pyramid, which leads to the unfinished tomb, alone is 119 meters long sloping downward through the rock at an angle (1.20 meters high and 1.06 meters wide, with an angle of inclination of 26° 31' 23"). How, actually, was this shaft made? **(Image 164)** By digging, chiselling away, of course. The first worker of the column must have pushed the lumps of rock, laboriously quarried with soft copper or iron chisels, behind him like a mole so that his fellow workers could transport the rubble outside. Only a *single man* could have worked in the shaft with its height of 1.20 meters and width of 1.06 meters. There was no room beside or above him. The deeper the shaft descended, the darker it became. So torches, wax, oil lamps were required and with them went the last bit of oxygen. At some point the human voles reached the spot at which the subterranean chamber was to be created. So onward as before—with chisels and hammers. Light and air were probably superfluous in the depths. Perhaps the teams were working in the dark with radar and Albino eyes and were not bothered by the chunks of rock which thumped one or the other of them on the head every so often, squashed fingers or trapped feet. **(Images 165–168)** The spoil was

162

carted to the surface on sledges, and presumably air was pumped into the caves full of stone dust with hoses made from animal intestines. Once the underground hall had been halfway excavated, the happy workers must have created the 15-meter-long, dead-end passage in the southwest corner just for the fun of it, which they then proceeded to line with polished blocks. As a parting gift, they dug a 3.5-meter-long hole in the ground, left the half-finished space behind, and began to line parts of the previously laboriously dug shaft with finely polished, massive blocks from Tura. More than 100 meters without the slightest deviation in inclination in a straight line upward. Hard to think that this subterranean work was carried out when the pyramid had already been built. Why not? Because the entrance to the 119-meter-long diagonal shaft starts in the pyramid. A contradiction? No. If the pyramid had already been standing when the excavations began, all the dirt would have had to be transported from the 119-meter-long shaft and the unfinished chamber **(Images 169–170)** into the pyramid. It would have had to be taken to the point where the ascending and descending passageways intersected and from there onwards to the actual entrance of the

163

pyramid 16.5 meters above the ground. Hence I assume that the 119-meter-long passage and the "unfinished tomb" were excavated first and only then were the first layers of the pyramid laid down. Although even at this point, the structure would already have had to have been planned exactly because the 119-meter shaft leads precisely into the pyramid.

I hear that the foreman changed during construction, or the pharaoh altered the plans on short notice. Excuse me? For as long as stones had to be quarried out of the rock down in the "unfinished tomb" and brought to the surface, the 119-meter shaft could not be lined with polished blocks from Tura. Even the first 10 meters of such a lining would have prevented the spoil from being transported away from the *cavern lying beneath*. There would have been no space—I did, after all, crawl down there—and the transport of the stones would have scratched the squeaky clean walls. Nothing like that can be seen, just as there are no wheel tracks or drag marks.

165

166

167

And what was it all for? For a space 35 meters vertically below the pyramid which no one needed.

Every shaft, be it ever so small, every ceiling of pink granite from Aswan, every passageway to a chamber, every upright or horizontal monolith of different a size was a part of a plan which was *finished and completed before the pyramid was built*. Changes during construction were not possible. The 60-meter-long Gantenbrink shaft could not be added afterward. Just think of the little door at the end of the shaft that finally led to a chamber. I also read some fool suggesting that the Gantenbrink shaft had been chiselled out of the pyramid blocks *after* the building was already long completed. That makes someone like me crazy! The Gantenbrink shaft has a side length of precisely 14 centimeters. Not even a Lilliputian team would fit in there after the event.

This shaft ends in a chamber which was discovered by the Djedi robot. So it was planned in advance. Furthermore, the builders seem to have known that only a high-tech society would be able to reach this chamber—thanks to robots. Any previous society would have had to dismantle the whole pyramid from top to bottom in order to reach the "Djedi chamber."

168

The planning of the Great Pyramid—I deliberately exclude the Chefren pyramid—the calculations, drawings, the knowledge about material thickness, the engineering work as a whole, does not fit in any way into the society of the Fourth Dynasty. Sneferu, the father of Cheops, came straight out of the Stone Age. The Cheops generation could only just about master iron and copper. To suggest that they had precisely planned the pyramid with its chambers, passageways, shafts, and different types and sizes of stone before building began makes about as much sense as a hippopotamus on the moon. The monoliths used inside the pyramid are of different lengths and widths, have different qualities and colors, depending on where they were used. The pink granite in the King's Chamber comes from Aswan, almost 1,000 miles away from the building site. Did they send sprinters to Aswan when a monolith crumbled and had to be replaced? And—please note—work was going on in the Fourth Dynasty at several building sites simultaneously. Monoliths were polished, quarried from the rock, transported on rafts and by cable haulage, and inserted in the right spot. This Fourth Dynasty may have done all kinds of things—but planning a pyramid with its complex inner life was beyond their capacities. This definitely does not

169

fit into the evolution of technology as it applied to Mr. Cheops' Fourth Dynasty. And such a statement can only be made today, now that we know about some of the confusing advanced technology inside the pyramid.

Every structure *before* Cheops should be even more primitive from a technical and planning perspective—so says evolution. Does that rule out any builder before Cheops?

Saurid (alias Enoch) is said to have built this miracle of construction before the Flood, ancient Arab historians claim. Why? To protect the all the knowledge of humankind from the Flood. The *Hitat* puts it like this:

> Thereupon he [the builder] had 30 vaults built in the western pyramid made of colored granite. They were filled with devices and ornamented columns made of precious gems, with equipment made of excellent iron such as weapons which did not rust, with glass which can be folded without breaking, with strange talismans.... In the eastern pyramid he had the different celestial vaults and planets represented and pictures made of what his

ancestors had created; in addition there was incense which was offered up to the stars and books about them. Also to be found there are the fixed stars and what arises in their periods from time to time.... Neither was there any science which he did not have written down and recorded. He further had transported there the treasures of the stars as well as the treasures of the prophets, and they formed a mighty and uncountable quantity....[39]

For decades, Enoch was the personal pupil of those types he called "heavenly guardians." To him they were not gods. He learnt their language and served as interpreter. He was taught writing, and the "heavenly guardians" dictated countless books to Enoch—scientific works about astronomy, geology, metallurgy, and so on. Enoch even revealed the names of his teachers. *We know* what those ETs were called and who was responsible for what area of studies. (Detailed information can be found in *Falsch Informiert*.[40])

Then the "heavenly guardians" informed Enoch that they would take him with them on their further journey "into heaven" (space) and that he should take leave of his family. Enoch followed the advice and told his son Methuselah: *"And now my son Methuselah.... I have told you everything and given you the books which concern all these things. Take good care of these books from your father's hand, my son Methuselah, and give them to future generations after the Flood..."*[41] (Emphasis by Erich von Däniken)

These few sentences clarify a number of things. Methuselah was Enoch's son ("and now *my son* Methuselah...from *your father's hand*...") Enoch speaks in the first person ("*I* have told you everything..."). The event takes place before the Flood ("give them to future generations *after the Flood*..."). We know for certain that Methuselah is the son of Enoch from the so-called Lamech Scroll (one of the Dead Sea Scrolls).[42] Enoch gave his son more than 300 books. Where are they, actually? There is nothing apart from the Ethiopic and Slavonic Book of Enoch and a number of fragments.

The *Hitat* records that God personally had instructed Saurid (alias Hermes, alias Enoch) in astronomy and had told him that a catastrophe would strike the earth. That fits Enoch to a T. He was meant to build the pyramid "to keep in it books of science and knowledge and other valuable

171

objects."[43] And Al-Mamun, who was the first to break into the pyramid, is said to have found books in an unknown writing in it, among other things. Were the Arab historians chasing shadows thousands of years ago?

Herodotus reports in the second book of his *Histories* that there was a lake with glassy water under the pyramid which had a sarcophagus in it. A phantom? A figment of someone's imagination? The lake has meanwhile been discovered. Plus the sarcophagus. **Images 171–174** prove it. No figment of the imagination. The reports of the ancient scribes were based on the best sources of information.

Are the original books of Enoch lying somewhere in the labyrinth of the alleged Cheops pyramid? Was it that the people did the dirty work of construction, gave their sweat, blood, and lives—but the planning was done by Enoch's teachers? They in turn knew about the coming Flood. After all, they not only informed the Biblical Noah but also in detail their pupil Enoch and their favorite Utnapishtim in the Gilgamesch epic.[44] In this line of thought, Enoch's "heavenly guardians" would have deliberately created

172

a building to survive the Flood and the following millennia. A building, moreover, that would always catch the eye of all terrestrial generations—a wonder of the world that would cause human beings to be amazed and enchanted, and lead them to investigate it further, a pyramid filled with geological, mathematical, and astronomical references. (There is a wealth of outstanding literature on these subjects. For mathematicians, for example, the book *Henochs Uhr* (Enoch's Clock) by Paul Krannich.[45]) A building with such a sophisticated inner life that it would require a high-tech society to discover the hidden spaces. A chronological treasure that would transport the information arising from Enoch's experiences and his contact with the ETs safely into the future. A future, by the way, in which the "gods" intended to return. Will we find not just books and technologies in the Great Pyramid but also the interstellar home addresses of those extraterrestrials who instructed the human being Enoch thousands of years ago?

173

I am clearly not the only person to pose such questions. For quite a while, measurements have been undertaken in the Great Pyramid using the most modern technology. There has even been crude drilling using pneumatic drills without the public being told a word about it. The untiring Alireza Zarei reports:

> When I visited the Giza plateau in 2009, I was able...to visit the relief chambers on several occasions. I reached the entrance to the relief chambers after climbing a temporary 8-meter ladder. I crawled straight towards the southwest corner to verify for myself a new, illegally dug tunnel. And it was indeed so! The original passage had been extended by some meters and turned sharply to the right at the end. There the passage continued in a straight line for another few meters where it ended in a barely 1.5 meter deep hollow. The use of modern tools could clearly be seen on the walls as the drag marks there were quite different from those in the Caviglias tunnel and the others in the pyramid.[46]

Alireza Zarei's **Images 175–177** prove what he saw.

No one drills in the Great Pyramid, and even less so with heavy equipment, without the knowledge of the authorities. The inspired structure is guarded around the clock. Someone must logically have come to an agreement with the Ministry of State of Antiquities. No heavy drills get into the Great Pyramid without explicit agreement. Which secret service might be involved? Who on our planet is so influential that even the duty of care of the archaeologists is grossly ignored? After all, the drills used could destroy valuable treasures. What is actually being sought? Just consider the huge effort in total secrecy. And my questions are not about conspiracy theories. Because if the drilling had been carried out officially, the public and our noble archaeologists could have been informed. Period!

Every tourist who gasps their way up the Grand Gallery inside the pyramid in amazement will notice metal brackets between the monoliths. What were they originally for? This miracle of construction today presents itself in total anonymity. Nothing, not a tiny little glyph, adorns this phenomenal complex. Why, then, the brackets?

Image 178 is the creation of my imagination. It shows the walls of the Grand Gallery as they might have looked millennia ago. Then someone came along and ripped the messages from the "heavenly guardians" (Enoch) off the walls. Human beings were not to venerate foreign gods,

175

176

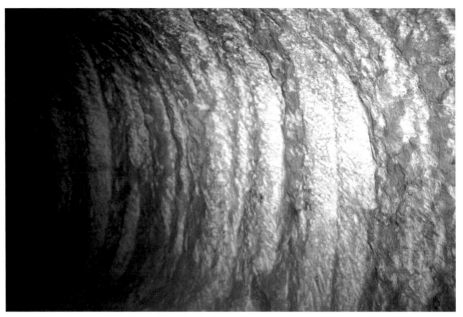

177

were not to find out who the original teachers of our young humanity were. Such knowledge would destroy the foundations of the great religions, be it Judaism, Christianity, or Islam. Those in the know in all religions are agreed on that. And because national politicians have close connections with the respective religions, the mystery-mongers, the pseudo responsibly minded in world politics are also told about it. Peoples of the world, unite in ignorance!

178

NOTES

Impossible Buildings

1. Heyerdahl, Thor. *Wege übers Meer*. Munich, 1975.

2. von Hassler, Gerd. *Noahs Weg zum Amazonas*. Hamburg, 1976.

3. Cajus Plinius Secundus. *Die Naturgeschichte*. Translated by Prof. Dr. G.C. Wittstein. Volume 1. Leipzig, 1881.

4. Homer. *Illias und Odysse*. Translated by Peter von der Mühll. Basel, 1946.

5. Mooney, George, W. *The Argonautica of Apollonius Rhodius*. Dublin, 1912.

6. Leisner, Georg and Vera. *Die Megalithgräber der Iberischen Halbinsel*. Berlin, 1943.

7. Kreuzer, Gottfried and Christine. *Die Felsbilder Südandalusiens*. Stuttgart, 1987.

8. Topper, Uwe. *Das Erbe der Giganten*. Olten, 1977.

9. Ibid.

10. von Däniken, Erich. *Prophet der Vergangenheit*. Düsseldorf, 1979.

11. von Däniken, Erich. *Die Spuren der Ausserirdischen*. Munich, 1990.

12. Knörr, Alexander. "Neues von den Cart Ruts auf Malta und Gozo." *Sagenhafte Zeiten*, No. 6/2009, Volume 11.

13. Schubert, André. "Als die Steine noch weich waren." *Sagenhafte Zeiten*, No. 3/2011, Volume 13.

14. Thom, A. and Thom, A.S. *Megalithic Remains in Britain and Brittany*. Oxford, 1978.

15. Knörr, Alexander. *Hagar Qim: auf den Spuren eines versunkenen Kontinentes*. 2007.

16. Micallef, Paul I. *Der prähistorische Tempel Mnajdra—ein Kalender aus Stein*. Malta, 1991.

17. Hausdorf, Hartwig. "Göbekli Tepe—Die älteste Stadt der Welt?" In: Conference volume of the AAS Berlin 2011. Gross-Gerau ,2012.

18. *Die Heilige Schrift des Alten und des Neuen Testaments*. Stuttgart, 1972.

19. Riessler, P. *Altjüdisches Schrifttum ausserhalb der Bibel. Die Apokryphe des Abraham*. Augsburg, 1928.

20. Ibid.

21. Ibid.

22. von Däniken, Erich. *Die Steinzeit war ganz anders*. Munich, 1991.

23. von Däniken, Erich. *Grüsse aus der Steinzeit*. Rottenburg, 2010.

24. Watkins, Alfred. *The Old Straight Track*. London, 1970.

25. Fester, Richard. *Protokolle der Steinzeit*. Munich, 1974.

26. Devereux, Paul and Robert Forrest. "Straight Lines on an Ancient Landscape." *New Scientist*, 23/30 December 1982.

Crazy Facts

1. Bedal, Karl: *Rätselhafte Verbindungen zwischen vorgeschichtlichen Fundstätten, Bodendenkmälern, Burgen und Kirchen.* 1993.

2. Ibid.

3. Ibid.

4. Ibid

5. Guichard, Xavier. *Alesia Eleusis. Entquête sur les origines de la civilisation européenne*. Paris, 1936.

6. Courlet, Louis. *La Cité Mystérieuse*. Alaise, 1999.

7. Jellinek, K. *Moses ben Schemtob von Leon*. Leipzig, 1851.

8. Fiebag, P., E. Gruber, and R. Holbe. *Mystica*. Augsburg, 2002.

9. Ibid.

10. Herodot. *Historien*. Munich n.y.

11. von Däniken, Erich. *Prophet der Vergangenheit*. Düsseldorf, 1979.

12. von Däniken, Erich. *Die Steinzeit war ganz anders*. Munich, 1991.

13. von Däniken, Erich. *Grüsse aus der Steinzeit*. Rottenburg, 2010.

14. Manias, Theophanis, N. *Die geometrisch-geodätische Triangulation des altgriechischen Raumes.* Athens, 1970.

15. Manias, Theophanis, N. *La triangulacion geometrico-geodésica des espacio de la antigua Grecia.* Madrid, 1971.

16. Manias, Theophanis, N. *The Invisible Harmony of the Ancient Greek World and the Apocryphal Geometry of the Greeks.* Edition of National Institution. Athens, 1969.

17. Rogowski, Fritz. "Tennen und Steinkreise in Griechenland." *Mitteilungen der Technischen Universität Carolo-Wilhelmina zu Braunschweig.* Braunschweiger Hochschulbund, Volume VIII/2/ 1973.

18. Runde, Ingo. "Griechenlands geheimnisvolle Geometrie." *Ancient Skies*, Volume 11, no. II. Feldbrunnen/Schweiz 1987.

19. Neugebauer, O. *The Exact Sciences in Antiquity.* University Press: Rhode Island, 1970.

20. Richter, Jean: *Géographie sacrée du Monde Grec.* Paris, 1983.

21. Plato. *Timaios.* Translated by Otto Apelt, 1922. New edition Hamburg, 1988.

22. Pannick, Nigel. *Die alte Wissenschaft der Geomantie.* Munich, 1982.

23. Cathie, Bruce. *Harmonic 33.* London, 1980.

24. Cathie, Bruce. *Harmonic 695.* London, 1981.

25. Morrison, Tony. *Pathways to the Gods.* Salisbury/Wiltshire, 1978.

26. Cobo, Bernabé. *Historia del Nuevo mundo.* 2 volumes. Madrid, 1953 and 1956.

27. Zuidema, Rainer Tom. *The Ceque-System of Cuzco.* Haarlem, 1962.

28. Denevan, William M. *The Aboriginal Cultural Geography of the Llanos de Mojos of Bolivia*. Los Angeles, 1966.

29. von Däniken, Erich. *Im Namen von Zeus*. Munich, 1999.

30. Feyerabend, Paul. *Naturphilosophie*. Frankfurt/M, 2009.

31. Ibid

32. Lovelock, Jim, E. *Unsere Erde wird überleben*. Munich, 1982.

33. Aram, Kurt. *Magie und Zauberei in der alten Welt*. Berlin, 1927.

34. Widengren, G. *Hochgottglaube im alten Iran*. Leipzig, 1938.

35. Kanjilal, Dileep, K. *Vimana in Ancient India*. Calcutta, 1985.

36. von Däniken, Erich. *Habe ich mich geirrt*? Munich, 1985 (Contribution by Prof. Dr. Kanjilal p. 225 ff.).

37. Kanjilal, Dileep, K. *Vimana in Ancient India*. Calcutta, 1985.

38. "Kebra Nagast: Die Heiligkeit der Könige." Abhandlung der Philosophisch-Philologischen Klasse der Königlich Bayrischen Akademie der Wissenschaften. Volume 23, 1st division. Munich, 1905.

39. Ibid.

40. Al-Mas'udi. *Bis zu den Grenzen der Erde*. Tübingen/Basel, 1978.

41. Huxley, Aldous. *Brave New World*. New York, 1965.

42. Bracewell, R.N. *The Galactic Club: Intelligent life in Outer Space*. San Francisco, 1975.

43. Deardorff, J.W. "Examination of the Embargo Hypothesis as an Exploration of the Great Silence." *Journal of the British Interplanetary Society*, 40, 1987.

44. Kean, Leslie. *UFOS. Generäle, Piloten und Regierungsvertreter brechen ihr Schweigen.* Rottenburg, 2012.

45. Ibid.

False Doctrines

1. Biffiger, Beat and Lothar Stanglmeier. *Der Kopf des Osiris.* (Unpublished research for the Erich von Däniken Foundation. 2004).

2. Naville, Edouard. *The Cemeteries of Abydos.* London, 1914.

3. Jeremis, Alfred. *Die ausserbiblische Erlösererwartung.* Leipzig, 1927.

4. Sethe, Kurt. Übersetzung und Kommentar zu den altägyptischen Pyramidentexten. Volume II. Darmstadt, 1922.

5. Ibid.

6. Faulner,R.O. *The Ancient Egyptian Pyramid Texts.* Oxford, 1969.

7. Burgard, Hermann. "Aratta—Jirof: Wiege der Kultur?" *Sagenhafte Zeiten* No. 2/2011, Volume 13.

8. Burgard, Hermann. *Encheduanna—Geheime Offenbarungen.* Gross-Gerau 2012.

9. Ibid.

10. Kanjilal, Dileep, K. Vimana in Ancient India. Calcutta, 1985.

11. Eggebrecht, Eva. "Die Geschichte des Pharaonenreiches." *Das alte Ägypten.* Munich, 1984.

12. Kees, Hermann: *Kulturgeschichte des Alten Orients.* Ägypten. Munich, 1965.

13. Diodor von Sizilien: *Gschichts-Bibliothek*. Book 1. Stuttgart, 1866.

14. Cajus Plinius Secundus. *Die Naturgeschichte*, Book 36. Leipzig, 1882.

15. Al-Maqrizi. *Das Pyramidnkapitel in Al-Makrizi's "Hitat."* Translated by Dr. Erich Graefe. Leipzig, 1882.

16. Ibid.

17. Ibid.

18. Tompkins, Peter. *Cheops*. Bern, 1975.

19. von Däniken, Erich. *Falsch informiert*. Rottenburg, 2007.

20. Schmöckel, Hartmut. "Die Himmelfahrt Henochs. Neue Aufschlüsse aus Keilschriften." *FAZ* No.159, 12 July 1973.

21. Kautsch, Emil. *Die Apokryphen und Pseudepigraphen des Alten Testaments*. Volume II, Tübingen, 1900. *Das Buch Henoch.*

22. Zarei, Alireza. *Die verletzte Pyramid*. Gross-Gerau, 2011.

23. Herodot: Historien. Munich n.y.

24. Cajus Plinius Secundus. Die Naturgeschichte. Translated by Prof. Dr. G.C. Wittstein. Volume 1. Leipzig, 1881.

25. Schüssler, Karlheinz. *Die ägyptischen Pyramiden: Erforschung, Baugeschichte und Bedeutung.* Köln, 1983

26. Al-Maqrizi. *Das Pyramidnkapitel in Al-Makrizi's "Hitat."* Translated by Dr. Erich Graefe. Leipzig, 1882.

27. Helck, Wolfgang. *Untersuchungen zu Manetho und den Ägyptischen Königslisten.* Berlin, 1956.

28. Pessl, H.V. *Das Chronologische System Manethos.* Leipzig, 1878.

29. Karst, Josef. *Eusebius Werke*, Volume 5. *Die Chronik* translated from the Armenian. Leipzig, 1911.

30. Zarei, Alireza. Die verletzte Pyramid. Gross-Gerau, 2011.

31. Yoshimura, Sakuji. *Non-Destructive Pyramid Investigation by Electromagnetic Wave Method*. Waseda University. Tokyo, 1987.

32. "Sphinx, Riddle put to Rest?" *Science*, Vol. 255, Nr. 5046, 14 February 1992.

33. "The Great Pyramid Mystery." *Mail on Saturday*, 17 April 1993.

34. "Portcullis blocks robot in Pyramid." *The Daily Telegraph*. 7 April 1993.

35. Telex Reuter und sda of 16 April 1993.

36. *SPIEGEL Online* of 29 May 2011.

37. *Mysteries* No. 21, Edition 4, 2011.

38. "Chefren-Pyramid—Fluch des Pharaos." *Der Spiegel*, No. 33, 1969.

39. Al-Maqrizi. Das Pyramidnkapitel in Al-Makrizi's "Hitat." Translated by Dr. Erich Graefe. Leipzig, 1882.

40. von Däniken, Erich. Falsch informiert. Rottenburg, 2007.

41. Kautsch, Emil. Die Apokryphen und Pseudepigraphen des Alten Testaments. Volume II, Tübingen, 1900. Das Buch Henoch.

42. Burrows, Millar. *Mehr Klarheit über die Schriftrollen*. Munich, 1958.

43. Tompkins, Peter. Cheops. Bern, 1975.

44. Burckhardt, Georg: *Gilgamesch*. Frankfurt, 1958.

45. Krannich, Paul H. *Henochs Uhr. Die Zeit der Giseh-Pyramiden.* Reppichau, 2009 (Books on demand, Norderstedt.).

46. Zarei, Alireza. Die verletzte Pyramid. Gross-Gerau, 2011.

INDEX

Abraham, 63, 67-68
  ascension of, 68
  legendary birthplace of, 63
Abydos,
  list of kings in, 153
  unknown origins of, 111
Alaise (place name), 73, 75, 80
  root of the word, 75, 80 (*see also*
  Elysium)
Alaise (village), 73, 75, 80
  as druid holy site, 75
Al-Mamum, Caliph Abdullah, 141,
  144
  Great Pyramid and, 144,
  157-158, 192
Al-Maqrizi, 147, 152 (*see also* Hitat)
Al-Mas'udi's *Histories*, 105
Alvarez, Louis, 177
Amélineau, Emile, 111
Antequera, 30

"anything goes" approach, 100 (*see
  also* Paul Feyerabend)
Apocalypse of Abraham,
  "heavenly beings" in the, 67-68
  spaceship in, 68
Apollo, 112
applied geometry, ancient examples
  of, 97
archeological misconception,
  classic case of, 44
Argonautica, 27
astronomical orientation
  of Mediterranean dolmens, 70
  of Mnajdra temple, 55-63
  of stone and wood circles, 51
Aswan granite, 122, 145, 186, 187
Avesta, 104
Babylonica, 104
Bacon, Sir Francis, 100
Battos, 33

Bavaria, network of lines in, 71-73

Bedal, Karl, 71, 72-73

Beethoven, Ludwig von, 80

Berossus, 104

Black, Henry, 97

Bracewell, Ronald, 108

Brave New World, 108

Britain, applied geometry in ancient, 97

Brittany, menhirs in, 68, 97

Burgard, Hermann, 121

Calais, 73, 75

Carnac, menhirs of, 97

Carthage, 12

Carthaginians, 9, 12

Cathie, Bruce, 97

Cerro de la Cruz, 33

Chefren pyramid, 163
    chaotic structure of, 179
    inexplicable phenomena in, 177
    radiation experiments in, 177, 179
    unsolved riddles in, 179

Cheops, 130
    as builder of the Great Pyramid, 146, 147, 154, 159, 162-163, 171
    father of, 141 (see also Sneferu)
    possibility of more than one, 162

Cheops pyramid, see Great Pyramid

Courlet, Louis, 80-81

crazy facts, 71-110

Cueva de Menga, 30 (see also Menga, Granada)

building materials of, 33

"burial chamber" of, 31, 33
    ceiling of, 31
    unknown origins of, 31

Cuevas del Rey Moro, 33 (see also Menga, Valencia)

Cyrene, 33

Damaged Pyramid, The, 153

Dead Sea Scrolls, 189

Deardorff, James, 108

Didorus of Sicily, 146

Dobecki, Thomas L., 171

dolmen,
    Hypogeum of Malta as different from any other, 51
    most impressive and best preserved, 30, 31

dolmens, Mediterranean, astronomical orientation of, 70

Dormion, Jean-Patrice, 171

Echo Flight Base, 109

Eden, 27

Eggebrecht, Eva, 130

Egypt,
    Great Pyramid of, 130-177, 179-200
    Manetho's list of rulers of ancient, 158-159
    myths of, 121
    Sphinx of, 171
    Sumer and, 121

ellipse of Mzora, 28
    unknown origins of, 30

Elysion, see Elysium

Elysium, 75, 80

England, megaliths in, 112

Enoch,
    as builder of the Great Pyramid, 152, 163, 188, 189, 192
    extraterrestrials and, 152, 189, 193
    "heavenly guardians" and, 189, 193
    meaning of the name, 152

Enoch's Clock, 193

Epic of Gilgamesh, 193

Etruscan cultic site, 81

Etruscans, 81
    Kabbalah and, 81
    knowledge of geometry of, 85
    origins of, 85

Euclid, 95-96

Europe,
    applied geometry in ley lines across, 97
    homogenous civilization in ancient, 75
    necessity of a comprehensive overview of, 44
    stone and wood circles in, 51

European anthem, 80 (*see also* "Ode to Joy")

evolution of technology, 9, 12, 63, 123, 126, 188

false doctrines, 111-200

Flood, the, 147, 152, 159, 163, 171, 188, 189, 192, 193

flying chariots, 105

flying machines, 105

France,
    applied geometry in, 97
    menhirs in, 51, 68 (*see also* Brittany and Carnac)
    network of lines in, 73, 75, 80-81
    place names in, 73, 75
    track-like grooves in southern, 44

Feyerabend, Paul, 100 (*see also* "anything goes" approach)

Gaius Plinius Secundus, 147

Gantenbrink, Rudolf, 171

Gantenbrink shaft, 177, 178, 186

Garden of Eden, 27

Gavrini, Island of, 51

Garden of the Hesperides, 12,
    nymphs and serpent in the, 27

grid, global, 97
    creators of, 97, 100
    facts, incomprehensible, 100

geometrical knowledge, original source of, 96

Germany, applied geometry throughout, 97

Göbekli Tepe,
    age of, 67
    description of, 63
    meaning of name, 63
    mystery of, 68
    reason for location of, 67-68
    reason for partial burying of, 67

Gohed, Amr, 179

Goidon, Gilles, 171

Goldener Schnitt, *see* golden ratio

golden ratio, 89, 92

Granada, 30

Granger, N. (*née* Tourtechot), 111

Great Pyramid, 130-177, 179-200
  absence of any inscription in, 157
  advanced technology inside, 188
  age of, 147
  anonymous nature of, 157
  builder of, 146, 147, 154, 163
  construction of, 130, 180, 182-183
  Enoch as builder of, 163, 188
  Grand Gallery in, 144
  hollow spaces in, 171, 176-177
  King's Chamber in, 145
  lake under, 192
  metal brackets in, 195
  metal fittings inside, 171, 176
  modern drilling in, 195
  planning of, 179, 183, 186-187
  possible contents of, 193, 195
  reason for construction of, 188, 192
  relief chambers in, 145-146
  robotic exploration of, 171, 173,
    176, 186
  salt crystals in, 171
  technology used to build, 137
  unfamiliar writing in, 158
  unknown writing in, 192

Greece,
  applied geometry over
    prehistoric temples in, 97
  survey points in, 104

Greek holy sites,
  geometrical relationship of, 85
  golden ratio and, 89, 92-94
  mathematicians of antiquity,
    95-96

mythology, 75
  sacred sites, megalithic origins
    of, 95-96

Greeks,
  ancient, geodetic surveying
    techniques of, 85
  prehistoric, surveying skills of, 97

grid squares, 108, 110

Guichard, Xavier, 73, 75

Hausdorf, Hartwig, 67

"heavenly beings" in the
  Apocalypse of Abraham, 67-68

"heavenly guardians," Enoch's, 152,
  189, 193
  messages from, 199

Hentschel, Peter, 81, 83, 85

Hermes, 147, 152 (*see also* Enoch)

Herodotus,
  opinion regarding the
    Etruscans, 85
  Great Pyramid and, 154, 156, 192

Heyerdahl, Thor, 12

Histories of Herodotus, 156, 192

history of technology, 141

Hitat, 147, 152, 158, 188-189

holy places, location of Franciscan, 85

holy site, druid, 75

holy sites,
  buried, 67
  Etruscan, 83
  geometrical arrangement of, 96
  Greek, geometrical relationship
    of, 85
  linear distances between, 81, 92

prehistoric, 75
straight lines connecting Stone
    Age, 68
Homer, 12
Huxley, Aldous, 108
hypogeum, definition, 51
Hypogeum of Malta, 51-63
    acoustics of, 55
    creators of, 51-52
    discovery of, 51
    other dolmen vs., 51
    perfect Megalithic style of, 51
    purpose of, 52
    Stone Age origins of, 51
Ibn Batutta, 152
impossible, suppression of the, 55
impossible buildings, 9-70
intercontinental missiles,
    immobilization of, 109
Italy,
    applied geometry in ancient, 97
    central, geometrical network in, 85
    mysterious lines in, 81-85
Julius Caesar, 75
Kabbalah, 81
    definition of, 83
    Tree of Life of, 81, 83, 85
Kabbalistic Tree of Life, *see* Tree of
    Life
Kanjilal, Dileep Kumar, 104-105
Kean, Leslie, 109
Kebra Nagast, 105
Kees, Hermann, 145
King Solomon, 105

Knörr, Alexander, 39, 55
Krannich, Paul, 193
Ladon, 27
land surveying, prehistoric, 97, 100,
    108
    means of, 101, 104
    reasons for, 108-110
    reason for ancestral, 97
ley lines, applied geometry in, 97
Libya, ancient tracks in, 33
Liks, 9, 27
Lixus, 9, 12, 28 (*see also* Liks)
    Garden of Eden and, 27
    megaliths of, 12
    mythological origins of, 27
    temple of Hercules and, 12
Malmstrom Air Force Base, 109
Malta,
    "Clapham Junction" in, 39
    Hypogeum of, 51-63
    lack of Flint on, 52
    temple of Mnajdra on, 55
    tracks/"cart ruts" around, 33, 39
    transnational nature of ancient, 44
Manetho, 158
Manias, Theophanias, 85, 89
Mariette, Auguste, 111
Mediterranean
    region, dolmens in, 70
    Sea, tracks in, 39
Megalithic yard, definition, 51
Megalithic structures
    in Morocco, 9-30

in Spain, 33
in Turkey, 63

Megalithic
    origins of Greek sacred sites, 95
    people, absurdity of the idea of
        a, 100
    ruin, 92
    structures, astronomical
        orientation of, 51
    style, perfect, 51
    temples, 55

megaliths
    of Lixus, 12
    of Stonehenge, 112

Menga (Granada), 30

Menga (Valencia),
    "tram network" and "rails"
        around, 33
    tracks around, 33

Methuselah, 189

Micallef, Paul, 55

Morocco, megalithic structures in,
    9-30

Moses Ben Schemtob de Leon, 83

most obvious solution, the, 94-95

Murray, Margaret, 111

Natural History, 12

Naville, Edouard, 111-112

network of lines, global nature of, 97

Neugebauer, Reimund, 96

Novum Organum, 100

Oannes, 104

original teaching, necessity of an, 159

Orion, 112

Osiris, 112 (*see also* Orion)
    as an extraterrestrial, 113
    head of, 113
    myth of, 112-113

Osireion, 111-113, 122-123, 126, 130
    as comparable with megaliths of
        Stonehenge, 112
    evolution of technology and, 126
    gods as builders of the, 122
    purpose of, 126, 130
    reason for name of, 112

Paradise, 27 (*see also* Eden)

Petrie, Sir Flinders, 111

Phoenicians, 9, 12

Piri Reis, 100

Plato, 95, 96, 104

Platonic vs. Euclidean geometry, 96

Pliny the Elder, 12, 157

preconceptions, necessity of
    jettisoning, 100

pyramid plateau, evidence of water
    on, 162-163

pyramids of Egypt,
    ancient descriptions of, 146-147,
        152, 154, 156-157, 158
    reason for building, 152

Pyramid Texts, 113
    modern interpretation of, 113, 121

Pythagoras, 68

Pythagorean triangles, 68, 97

Rathas, meaning of, 105

Red Cross, 71

Richter, Jean, 96

religious culture, origins of, 63

Rigveda, 105

Rogowski, Fritz, 94

Romans, 12, 28

sacred sites, Greek, megalithic origins of, 95-96

Salas, Robert, 109

Sardinia, tracks around, 33

Saurid, 147 (*see also* Enoch and Hermes)
    as builder of the Great Pyramid, 147, 189, 192

Schiller, Friedrich, 80

Schoch, Robert M., 171

Schubert, André, 43

Sephirot, 83

Simon Bar Jochai, Rabbi, 83

simple probability, principle of, 94 (*see also* most obvious solution)
    pitfalls of, 94-95

Sneferu (ruler), 141

Sneferu (pyramid), erosion on, 163

Spain,
    megalithic structures in, 30-31, 33
    tracks in, 33

Sphinx, age of, 171

Stone Age
    ancestors, categorization of our, 63
    architecture, 33
    foundations of the temple of
        Apollo, 94
    holy sites, 68
    points, Bavarian, 71

settlement, underwater, 75
    structure, 31
    thinking, 51

Stone Age,
    reason for term, 52
    use of Flint during, 52
    use of metals during, 52

Stone Age Was Quite Different, The, 97

stone and wood circles, astrological orientation of, 51

Stonehenge, 112

Strait of Gibraltar, 9

Sumer, Egypt and, 121

Sumerian
    King List, 152, 159
    myth, 121

"super galactic communities" hypothesis, 108 (*see also* Ronald Bracewell)

survey of Antarctica, 97, 100 (*see also* Piri Reis)

surveying skills,
    Etruscan, 85
    prehistoric Greek, 97

surveying techniques, ancient Greek, 85

Tangier, 9

Temple Hymns of Enheduanna, 121
    appropriate contemporary translation of, 122
    descriptions of technology in, 121-122

Timaeus, 96, 104

Topper, Uwe, 33

Tourtechot, *see* Granger

tracks, ancient, 33-47
    author's opinion regarding, 43-44
    possible sources of, 43
    timeframe of, 44
    underwater, 39, 43

Tree of Life, 81, 83, 85

Turkey, megalithic structures in, 63

Tuscany,
    image of the Tree of Life in, 83
    network of lines in, 81-85, 97
    system of equilateral triangles
        in, 83

UFO phenomenon, our impotence
    with regard to, 109

*UFOs: Generals, Pilots and
    Government Officials Break Their
    Silence*, 109

Viracocha, 112

von Hassler, Gert, 12

wind rose system, 75

Yma, 104

Zarei, Alizera, 153, 171, 195

"zoo hypothesis," 108-109 (*see also*
    James Deardorff)

zoo, monitoring of the, 108-110

ABOUT THE AUTHOR

Born on April 14, 1935, in Zofingen, Switzerland, **Erich von Däniken** was educated at the College St. Michel in Fribourg, where he was already occupying his time with the study of ancient holy writings. While working as managing director of a Swiss 5-star hotel, he wrote his first book, *Chariots of the Gods,* which was an immediate bestseller in the United States, Germany, and, later, in 38 other countries. He won instant fame in the United States as a result of the television special *In Search of Ancient Astronauts,* which was based on that book. His other books, including the more recent *Twilight of the Gods* and *Odyssey of the Gods,* have been translated into 32 languages and have sold more than 63 million copies worldwide.

From his books, two full-length documentary films have been produced, *Chariots of the Gods* and *Messages of the Gods.* As well, the History Channel is continuing its extremely successful series *Ancient Aliens,* for which Giorgio A. Tsoukalos, of the Center for Ancient Astronaut Research and publisher of *Legendary Times Magazine,* serves as consulting producer.

Of the more than 3,000 lectures that Erich von Däniken has given in 25 countries, more than 500 were presented at universities. Fluent in four languages, Erich von Däniken is an avid researcher and a compulsive traveler, averaging 100,000 miles each year to the most remote spots on the globe. This enables him to closely examine the phenomena about which he writes. Erich von Däniken is a member of the Swiss Writers Association, the German Writers Association, and the International PEN Club. He was awarded with an honorary doctorate degree by the La Universidad Boliviana. He received the Huesped Illustre award from the cities of Ica and Nazca in Peru. In Brazil, he received the Lourenço Filho award in Gold and Platinum, and in Germany he was awarded with the Order of Cordon Bleu du Saint Esprit (together with the German astronaut Ulf Merbold). In 2004, he was awarded the Explorers Festival prize.

In 1998, Erich von Däniken cofounded the Archaeology, Astronautics, and SETI Research Society (AASRS), which publishes the English journal *Legendary Times*, reporting on the latest research in the paleo-SETI field. In 2003, he opened his "Mysteries of the World" theme park in Interlaken, Switzerland, which still fascinates visitors with his research into the various mysteries of the world, including paleo-SETI and the Ancient Astronaut Theory.

Today, Erich von Däniken lives in the small mountain village of Beatenberg in Switzerland (40 miles from Berne, above the city of Interlaken). He has been married to Elisabeth Skaja since 1960. He has one daughter, Cornelia (born 1963), and two grandchildren. Von Däniken is an amateur chef and a lover of Bordeaux wines.